CW01494696

Acknowledgement of Country

We acknowledge the traditional custodians on the lands on which we work and on which this book was produced, and pay our respects to Elders past, present and emerging. We recognise that sovereignty was never ceded. Always was always will be. Aboriginal land.

We embrace the principle of 'First Nations First': re-centring Australian history with Indigenous histories. We recognise that Australia's migration history began, and continues, on stolen land that has not been ceded; and that it is untenable to talk about race in Australia without situating it in the histories of dispossession and colonisation of Australia's First Peoples.

AFTER AUSTRALIA

Affirmpress
books that leave an impression

Published by Affirm Press in 2020 in partnership with Diversity Arts Australia in association with Sweatshop Literacy Movement Inc.

After Australia was developed as part of the larger *Stories from the Future* project, which is an initiative of, and managed by Diversity Arts Australia.

28 Thistlethwaite Street, South Melbourne, VIC 3205
www.affirmpress.com.au
10 9 8 7 6 5 4 3 2 1
Copyright © this collection Diversity Arts Australia and Affirm Press 2020
Individual stories copyright © retained by individual copyright holders
All rights reserved. No part of this publication may be reproduced without prior permission of the publisher.

 A catalogue record for this book is available from the National Library of Australia

Title: After Australia / Edited by Michael Mohammed Ahmad
ISBN: 9781925972818
Cover design by Design by Committee
Typeset in Granjon 12 /19 by Affirm Press
Proudly printed in Australia by Griffin Press

The paper this book is printed on is certified against the Forest Stewardship Council® Standards. Griffin Press holds FSC® chain of custody certification SGS-COC-005088. FSC® promotes environmentally responsible, socially beneficial and economically viable management of the world's forests

After
Australia

Edited by Michael Mohammed Ahmad

The future belongs to those who prepare for it today.

— Malcolm X

Contents

Black Thoughts

Unreconciliatory Futures

Hannah Donnelly

I'm gonna educate you gronks. I get pissed off when white people wear the Aboriginal flag. Hey you, yeah I'm talking to you. At protests, at exhibition openings, in selfies on Invasion Day, or because you lived in the Northern Territory for five years. I don't think there is ever a time in space for white bearers of the Koori flag. I should say Aboriginal flag cause south-east Aboriginal people, we don't own the flag. I had a Noongar housemate once who would always get annoyed when it came up and say, 'Yeh, you mean the Noongar flag.'

I used to have a sticker of the flag on my old red two-door Holden Barina. At the bottom, it said: one mob. I remember this footy head I hooked up with at the Koori Knockout laughed when he spotted it. 'Why do you have that sticker on your car?' Maybe, like so many others, he decided he was more black than me so he could laugh at my existence. Maybe he was just freaked out that I was parking my car out the front of his place when I stayed over and now his cousins knew he was sleeping with an Aboriginal woman and his masc Aboriginal self was disturbed. I don't know. He probably just wanted to make a Bob Marley reference, *one love one mob*.

After he pointed it out though, whenever I jumped in the car, the flag loomed large. It weighed on me so much that I started to think it must be weighing on everyone, and that a redneck with Southern Cross mudflaps would see it one day and try to run me off the road. Months after I stopped sleeping with Footy Head cause he was too much of a bitch, I was driving down to Coffs Harbour. I parked in a standard concrete residential parking lot with hedges and steel fences. I was gonna leave my car there and get a lift with another friend further down the coast. As I started getting out, I heard a wheelie bin rumble. I saw this older guy in double plugger thongs and Union Jack boardies taking his bins out right next to the boot of my Barina. I thought nah I gotta peel that sticker off, this fucker is gonna do some shit to my car if he sees the flag. Once Double Plugger was gone, I picked at the edges of the sticker furiously with my nails and it came off in flaky pieces. There was a dusty, sticky outline of where the flag had been. That outline never went away.

Everyone thinks that the flag belongs to them, to us the people, but that's not really true. Since 1995, it's been recognised as an official flag of Australia under the Flags Act, but only one person owns the copyright: Luritja artist Harold Thomas. It was the era of the Tent Embassy and land rights activism, and it became a symbol of the black power movement here in Australia. The flag is what those activists needed for a united Aboriginal movement of many nations. Powerful stuff. Nowadays, the company that has exclusive rights to use the flag on apparel is co-owned by a man who got done for selling fake Aboriginal souvenirs through yet another company. That's capitalism in the colony for you: making money on what's real and what's fake without sparing a thought for the culture it represents.

It's as simple as etching three lines into any surface: one horizontal line, a circle followed by a horizontal line, some people might add two vertical lines to bracket the meaning. Either form is a secret message to the next blackfella who finds your scratchings. I was here. You are here. We are still here. And that's why the flag feels like ours when you wear it, no matter the copyright, or who profits, it's a pan-Aboriginal thing, not a tribal thing.

I read a rant on the internet that said Harold Thomas stole the design off another blackfella, let's call him Mr B, who was his student at a community college. Harold was eventually declared the owner of the copyright of this flag by the Federal Court. Two other people came forward to claim ownership of the copyright in 1997. Of course, one was a culture vulture white art student, and the other was Mr B. Over twenty years later Mr B was still trying to get what he thought was his due on the internet. When I read this viral post on Shitbook, I couldn't tell if it was just some right-wing troll on the other end of the flag rant. See, the internet is the place where the undefinable cultural authorities and the right-wing Nazis can become the same thing. Would you ever expect a black person and Andrew Bolt to say the same thing? No, but fuck me dead it happens – what happens when an emu and a lamington walk into a bar? Crickets.

I don't dispute that Harold Thomas designed the flag. I just find the internet does remarkable things to the truth. *Standing on sacred ground* living on syndicated capitalist time. *Solid Rock* was written by white people. Out of all the various possible realities, Australia is just a glitch.

There are t-shirts you can buy that say 'Free the Flag' cause Aboriginal people get cease-and-desists from the fake art company. There are still local councils that won't fly the Aboriginal flag and I haven't even mentioned the Torres Strait Islander flag yet – the TI flag is another official flag of Australia, designed by the late Bernard Namok, and the copyright is held by the Torres Strait Island Regional Council. The TI flag and the Aboriginal flag are like cousins when they fly proud together over rooftops and entrances.

I remember when I asked my high school principal if we could leave the Aboriginal flag up after NAIDOC Week finished, he choked on his reconciliation scone and said, 'We'll have to think about it,' while licking jam and cream from his lips. In my last year of school, the principal conceded to fly the flag outside of NAIDOC Week, but only on the condition that an Aboriginal student had to learn how to ceremoniously raise and lower the flag, and be responsible for doing it every day. I would get to the flagpole and raise my flag before the groundskeeper was able to raise the Aussie flag because I knew it was improper protocols and it would annoy the teachers. Black flag is black pride. I wear the black flag. I don't know what people see when I do. Possibly that I'm some unidentifiable minority with a Koori flag on. Maybe she's a quadroon. Maybe she's born with it. Maybe she's black black black.

we live on, in story

Karen Wyld

The wind settled. High-pitched howling replaced by a gentle murmur. She thought it sounded familiar. Like a warm lullaby she'd once heard. Tears spent, Lilith wiped her face with the hem of her dress. Listening to the wind, she recalled that she'd never had a lullaby sung to her, let alone felt the warmth of human kindness. Momentarily forgetting what had just happened up at the house, she was lulled by the wind, even though she knew this faint essence of a familiar song was just false memories taunting her again. She leant back on the tree trunk, feeling its strength flow up her spine. When younger, she thought this large gumtree was hollow and had searched for a hidden entrance. She spent a lot of time in this clearing, down by the river; whenever she felt lonely or wanted to escape Mrs Barton's sharp tongue for a few hours. Despite the closeness of the river, it was a barren patch of land, with the old gumtree in the centre. This tree had a deep, elongated scar; as if someone had cut a canoe shape in its wide trunk. She often talked to the tree, sharing secrets; happy moments, and what made her scared or sad. Things she'd say to her mother, if she could.

She got up slowly, fresh bruises making movement difficult. She had bolted out of the house when she'd heard

Mrs Barton call for Ted to fetch the rifle. Barefoot, with no possessions, Lilith was unexpectedly free at last. She listened to water flowing in the river and thought she might follow it, all the way to the sea. She'd overheard the seasonal workers' tales of seas. With one last look at Barton Homestead, she walked into the night, vowing to return one day, with lullabies for her boy. She asked both wind and tree to mind Johnny until then.

Jack Barton excused himself, expressing a need for air. As he stood on the wide verandah, he looked towards the old gumtree. Just a stump, no longer a tree. His grandfather had cut it down years ago, before Jack was born, at the insistence of Grandmother Mary. Jack's father, John, had told him stories of climbing that tree when he was young; hiding from his mother on the highest branches. Only once did young John fall. He'd broken an arm that day, which is probably why she'd demanded the tree be cut down.

Along with boyhood stories of solo adventures, exploring the country surrounding the family's homestead, his father had told him that tree was significant. He couldn't say why; it was just a feeling. Jack understood, as he felt safe whenever he was near that stump. The surrounding land caused a different feeling: disbelief and grief. Jack once again wished his father was still here. He hoped that pain would lessen with time. He moved towards the steps, intending to walk to the stump. Hearing his name called, he paused. With a deep sigh, he went back inside to mingle with guests at his engagement dinner.

She bit harder on her forearm, blood trickling from the self-inflicted wound. Flesh absorbing muffled cries of pain. Ignoring the kaleidoscope of sounds beyond her quickly made nest – rifles cracking, horses squealing in protest and upstanding citizens caught up in a blood-lust frenzy – she focused on the increasing contractions, biting down whenever the pain became too much. To make a sound could mean death. Hiding in the tree's cavity, she tried not to think of the jigsaw of images and sounds she'd just witnessed. She was thankful for the protection the wind provided and hoped it would blow the furious men away. This uncanny wind joined her, inside the tree. It swirled around, filling the cavity with warmth. She felt it gently touch her mind. The wind gathered the young woman's thoughts, filling up the hollow in the tree trunk with unspoken words. It asked for stories. So she shared tales that had been told to her by family, through the generations, and visiting storytellers. There was the one about how crow got its shiny blue-black feathers. Her favourite. And the yarn of when her father and Uncle fell into the water while trying to land the fattest fish ever seen in that part of the river. The wind listened, touching her bare skin occasionally, encouraging her to share more. She blushed when she told of how she'd met her fella. And then felt saddened when she realised he'd never hold their baby.

Swirling, twirling, the wind gathered words and stories. Still hungry, it asked for more. She told the wind of the boss-man and his woman. Short, stout and pale; both of them. They looked nothing like anyone in her family. All the newcomers were pale; white like the bones of long-dead animals. Boss-man made her kin work too hard, striking them with a whip if they dragged their feet. They weren't allowed to hunt white-man's fat beasts. The hooved beasts had slowly destroyed everything green, forcing the kangaroos to move away. There was a tinge of smoke on the wind, carried in from outside. She thought of freshly cooked meat and could almost feel warm fat running down her chin. Before the newcomers, there'd been lots of bushtucker. Now, Missus gave them flour to keep them strong enough to toil. They had to pick out the weevils before making damper. She also gave them tins of a sickly-sweet red paste to put on their damper. The young woman told the wind all those stories.

In return, the wind shared stories from the future. A glimpse of a lean, tall woman with an abundance of brown curls. This woman sat in a roughly built wattle-and-daub hut. The single room had two long rows of steel beds with lumpy pillows and scratchy blankets. The woman sang lullabies, surrounded by children. The wind showed a boy sitting on his mother's lap. He too had curly hair. His eyes were most catching: one blue, one brown. His mother crooned him to sleep. The wind fell silent and the images faded. The woman felt a mix of grief and hope. She put aside thoughts of rivers of red soaking into the earth, surrounding the tree, drowning her.

She whispered to the future, 'Can you hear, dearest one? These are our stories. Our language. The wind will keep them safe. Through these stories, we remember kin. And we will use them to fight for justice. We must never forget what happened today, on our land.'

She'd not heard him approach. She looked up, as the wind departed, and saw steel-blue eyes. Boss-man had found her.

He looked down at her in disgust. 'What have you done now, Rosie?'

Too tired to speak, she thought: *That's not my true name.* Pulling red-tinged steel from his boot, he leaned forward, into the tree's cavity. The wind had not warned her this was how her story ended. She spat in his face before biting the side of his hand. The infant arrived on a river of blood, mucus and story. Boss-man looked down in revulsion, at his boots, and the baby. Bending, knife in hand, he roughly severed the umbilical cord and scooped up the newborn.

Lilith shivered. It was always windy by the old gumtree, although usually not this cold. Sometimes she imagined that she could hear voices on the wind. As a child, she had pretended they were stories from the time when people like her had lived unencumbered, before the newcomers had arrived. She'd once heard a black stockman call these newcomers white devils. Once, after Mrs Barton had given her a belting for breaking the sugar bowl, Lilith called her a white devil. Mrs Barton gave her another smack, and said she had too much sin in her. She made Lilith kneel on the rough bricks outside the kitchen door and recite Bible verses until her voice was hoarse. She found comfort in knowing she was not a Barton. They treated her like a slave, not a daughter. She knew her real mother would've taught her how to hear stories on the wind.

'Can you hear me? Can you feel the stories?'

Startled, she looked around. She laughed at herself. She was almost fourteen. Too old for such childish fantasies. Reluctantly, she stood and walked toward the homestead, towards chores and Mrs Barton's constant criticism. Towards that new look in Mr Barton's eyes; a look that confused and scared her.

'Be alert,' whispered the wind. Too late. Lilith had already left.

Lily looked at the fading photos on the shelf above the fireplace. She had never felt comfortable in this old house and only visited because her grandparents could no longer make the trip into the city. Pop was hard of hearing now and often had a faraway expression on his face; as if listening to something no one else could hear.

'Lily asked you a question.'

'What, dear?' he said, turning to his wife.

Sally smiled and reached over, taking his hand, 'Your granddaughter is speaking to you.'

He looked at Lily and smiled. She was his daughter's only child and had always been a joy; even when she was being obstinate.

'Pop, how come Great-grandfather John looked nothing like his mother?'

'I once asked him. He said his parents had refused to talk to him about the matter.'

'He looked a bit like his father, and also not. In these sepia photos, Ted's eyes look very pale, so I'm guessing blue. Your eyes are similar to your father's brown eyes. I inherited Ted's blue eyes, and your trait for not getting sunburnt. Do we have Aboriginal heritage?'

'Maybe. My father believed that Mary Barton was not his biological mother. They looked nothing alike. Mary's fair skin blistered from brief exposure to sunlight. After she died of cancer, Ted shut himself away; leaving my father to care for himself. When he was fifteen, his father died, taking all family secrets with him. It would be good to find the skeletons.'

'Do you mind if I go through the boxes of old documents in the study? I might be able to find something.'

'Of course you may, but you will probably be disappointed.'

'Does that mean you're staying for a while?' asked Sally.

'If you don't mind. I can help organise Pop's birthday. Maybe we can make plans over a cuppa? I'll put the kettle on.'

'No sugar for either of us. The doctor has your pop on a strict diet.'

Jack grunted in disapproval. Glancing at her husband, Sally wondered if he'd noticed how radiant their grand-daughter was looking.

She'd been searching through old documents and staring at photos for days. Photos of Bartons who had come before her; ones she'd never met. Looking at the photos, she noticed more and more milk had been added to the tea. And then there was her. As a child, she'd hated being called olive. And the teasing; even though she hadn't been that different from the other girls at school.

She turned the pages of a large album. It was so old that the cover had fallen off when she'd first picked it up. She re-examined a sepia photo of Ted and Mary as newlyweds. Ted had sepia-brown hair and the beginnings of a moustache faintly visible above stern thin lips. He was seated on a short-maned stocky horse. In the background, on the steps of the homestead's verandah, stood Mary. Behind her, almost invisible, was a skinny girl in the shadows of the doorway. That same girl had appeared in a few photos; transitioning from child to adolescent. Lily turned the pages, flicking back to the beginning of the album. There was a photo of healthy, muscular Aboriginal men helping Ted build Barton Homestead. And then images of the same men; slightly older, tireder, thinner, driving clouds of sheep into pens made of logs. There was a photo of Aboriginal women hanging up sheets on long lines of rope, dogs and hens at their feet. In a couple of photos, there were campfires with people and scrawny dogs gathered around, eyes avoiding the camera lens; or maybe the person wielding the camera. In the second half of the album, there were no more photos of Aboriginal workers or families camping down by the river. Photos of the curly-haired girl appeared at that point in the collection, and stopped when she was a teenager. Lily was puzzled: *Where had all the Aboriginal people gone?*

Lily kept returning to an entry in one of Ted's journals, written 15th of May 1870. After reading it again, she left the house, hoping a walk would clear her thoughts. Sitting by the old tree stump, she tried to make sense of what she'd just read. It had been hard reading as some of it was callously graphic. She reflected on what Ted had written in his journal, trying to decide if she should tell Pop. His health had declined rapidly since the party. She'd been helping as much as she could, as both her grandparents were exhausted most days. She didn't want to add to their worries.

Leaf litter began to swirl a few metres away. She watched a small willy-willy take shape, her thoughts lulled by movement and sound. Leaning against the stump, she closed her eyes and rested a hand on her stomach, feeling a slight quiver. Lily knew she couldn't keep this secret from her parents and grandparents for much longer. She just needed time to accept that he wasn't coming back. She watched the twirling wind, feeling suddenly tired.

Drifting off, Lily saw two images: blood seeping from a bite-shaped wound on a man's hand; and a scarred hand grabbing a girl by the shoulder. Opening her eyes with a gasp, she thought again of the curly-haired girl in the photos. *Who was she?* Lily forced herself to remember every word she'd read in Ted's journal. He'd documented the events that had taken place on that bloody night. She could almost hear the sounds. At least a dozen settlers had become murderers. She looked back at the lavish homestead, vividly aware that it had been built on the blood, sweat and tears of people that had lived on this land for eons. She thought of one particular person Ted had killed: an unnamed woman who had given birth, alone, in this very spot.

'Can you hear me? Can you feel the stories?'

Lily thought she'd heard a woman's voice. Looking around, she saw no one. She had no choice. She had to show her pop the journal.

Liam ran into his mother's arms and, laughing, she hugged him tightly. As he nestled into her, Pearl breathed in the aroma of childhood adventure: gum leaves, mud and biscuit crumbs. She clicked her tongue at the state of his hair, running her fingers gently through his tangle of curls. He looked up at her, protesting. She smiled. He had such beautiful eyes: one blue, like his father's, one brown, like hers.

'Do you want a story?'

He shook his head. 'Uncle Leroy just gave me one. It wasn't as good as yours.'

She smiled, pleased her son appreciated stories. When she'd married James, she became part of the Centre. She worked in the library and ran the storytelling sessions. To her, stories were treasure – like the old lullabies that had been passed down through many generations and across fractured lines. James's uncle Leroy had been excited the first time he'd heard her singing lullabies to the baby. With her help, Leroy had traced the origin of the songs, proving that not everyone had been killed in the massacre. Now he was documenting what happened to Lilith, after she'd left Barton Homestead.

'Sing, Mum,' said Liam, snuggling in even closer. 'That one the lady sang whenever the children cried for their families.'

She thought of the times she'd been held tightly while someone sang to her. And how her heart would break, never to be repaired, if anyone took her child. She was glad those Home kids had Lilith to show them what love was. Pearl's great-grandmother had been one of those children. So she believed singing these lullabies to her son honoured those stolen or killed in the Frontier Wars. Sensing his rhythmic breath, she let him sleep.

Leroy gave the door a shove with his shoulder. It opened with a loud creak. Obviously, it had not been used for a very long time. The dust on the floor and cobwebs on the ceiling backed up this theory. He knew his mother hadn't been to the homestead since Great-grandfather Jack had died. Sally died shortly after, in a nursing home, a month after Leroy had been born. This was his first visit to the family's property; if one could call being amongst ghosts a visit. He and his younger sister were now the last Bartons. They were still grieving for Lily, who'd died in an accident in her newly restored vintage car. Leroy had been assisting his mother's research on the history of this place; breaking apart the Barton settlement tale to reveal the truth. His mother had often talked of her plans to heal the land he now stood on. It was up to him to finish what she'd started.

Leroy decided to inspect the house last. He was more interested in the land it stood on. He headed towards the large tree stump he'd noticed when driving up to the house. The ground he walked on was dry, and leaf litter crunched under his feet. He imagined how it might have looked before years of drought and dust storms had taken away the fertile topsoil. When he reached the stump, he sat down next to it. He couldn't even begin to imagine the violence that had taken place on this spot. And he understood why his sister hadn't felt ready to make this trip; especially so close to giving birth.

From studying the old documents, he knew this was where the massacre had taken place. An estimated sixty deaths. After, the river carried them out to sea. Ted had recorded these details as if mass murder was a minor incident. He'd listed the names of the guilty: a retired judge, three police officers, a few local lads, and a handful of indignant neighbours. The murders were sparked by collective outrage over the loss of nine sheep. These were later found on a distant neighbour's property, after the wrongly accused had been murdered.

The mystery of the unknown girl, from the photos, took longer to solve. Leroy had almost given up, until he saw an entry in a stock ledger. *March twenty-second in the year of 1855. Born: female. Birthplace: creek campsite. Dam: Rosie – deceased on March twenty-second '55. Sire: unknown. Name: Lilith. To be trained as a house-girl.* This information had led to Leroy and his mother finally uncovering another family secret: who was John's mother? A recording in the journal stated: *She delivered May fifteenth, 1870. The boy shows some resemblance. Mary is most unpleased. The girl will need to be sent off. A most unfortunate outcome, as she was a decent enough house-girl and not unpleasant to look at.* With those two findings, the girl in the photographs was finally revealed: Lilith, their maternal ancestor.

Leroy looked around the clearing. His mother had imagined two monuments here: a memorial for those killed in the massacre, and a statue of Lilith reunited with her mother and son. This would be combined with a regeneration project to restore the land. He once again noticed how dry this place was, and thought of how much work lay ahead. Selling the house would enable him to fulfil his mother's plans. He wanted to do more. He imagined a building full of light and colour, where people shared stories. He knew people, Elders and other experts, who wanted to help create a space for truth-telling of this country's past. And perhaps writing programs, to create stories that imagined a just future. He would have liked to work on language revival; so far, his research had indicated his people's language was gone. *His people*. Leroy still felt conflicted saying that. For as long as he could remember, his mother had read him and his sister stories from Aboriginal-authored books, and shown them documentaries. She had taken them to community events, and joined in cultural programs and political activism. His mother had also developed reciprocal relationships within local communities. Unfortunately, these connections could never replace what had been taken. When he'd momentarily became adrift as a younger man, his mother had told him that being honest about the Bartons' dark past, and the pain it caused, couldn't lessen their sense of pride in having deep roots in this country. Leroy still wasn't sure his mother had been right. He knew pride and the blood running through his veins, was not enough for him to respectfully claim Aboriginality. Those branches of the family tree had been hacked off. There was no one left to claim him, or properly introduce him to country.

He stood up and stretched. Walking to the river, he imagined what it might have looked like; clean, fresh water flowing towards the sea. He threw a rock in the shallow river, reflecting on events from long ago. He no longer identified as a Barton. Not after learning of the atrocities that Ted had committed: years of tormenting the sovereign people of this place, and the terrifying mass murder. He could not forgive Mary, either. Piecing together family and local stories, he quickly realised she'd been a cruel woman. She'd tormented Lilith, chasing her from the home and forcing her to leave behind her beloved son; then she raised John in a loveless home.

Leroy had accepted that he couldn't recover what his settler ancestors had taken from his Aboriginal ancestors. Instead, he would focus on bringing life back to the barren clearing and struggling river. This place could be healed. The wind picked up. He didn't feel cold, as there was a peculiar warmth coming from the old tree trunk he leaned against.

'Can you hear me? Can you feel the stories?'

Leroy paused, before whispering, 'Yes. Yes, I can.'

Bu
Liao
Qing

Michelle Law

At 10pm, I go to meet my mum at the markets, where the stench of rotting fish is so strong I need to hold my nose. I'm surprised and terrified to find several other women (some my age, with their mothers, but mostly older women with their partners or friends) at the dock. What if the crowd gives us away? But the mothers, partners, and friends … they don't seem to care anymore. Their time was always up in this country, and because of what they're enabling tonight, they'll likely be dead by morning. Some of them are crying; all of them are whispering.

'Be brave. Our ancestors survived the same and so can you.'

'Where women's bodies go, trouble follows. Stay safe.'

'Don't cry, I will love you forever.'

'Your Po Po guessed I was a girl, and that you were a girl. You have a girl in there.'

One by one, they step into the boat.

It takes me some time to spot my mum but the moon is bright tonight and soon I see her standing alone at the end of the jetty, tapping her foot and holding a fresh flask of herb soup tightly against her chest like a cushion. When I'm close enough to make out her face, I see that she is crying, and I gasp aloud.

She opens her mouth to speak and I hug her tightly, silencing her. A moment passes. Then she kisses me on the forehead and pushes me backwards into the boat with the flask of soup. I watch her walk into the dark night, back towards the train station. When she's out of view I stare into the open water, all those fish belly-up, and I vomit.

One morning Mum packs me a flask of herb soup and leads me to the front door, gripping my arm like I could topple at any moment. She rests her hand on the doorknob before I can reach it.

'You don't have to tell him,' she writes, and then erases. Most people use notepads, but we use small pieces of plastic packaging, the hardy stuff you need to cut through, because if we're ever inspected we can just say it's leftover rubbish. The plastic was Mum's idea; I guess you could call her clever, or paranoid, or both.

I don't respond, just pull on my boots and try ignoring the cramping feeling in my stomach. I make sure not to frown or rub the area; if I give anything away she'll stop me from going out at all. Mum watches me with her arms crossed, brow furrowed and squinting slightly; her glasses broke when an Official held her face down on the market floor when she got caught up in a riot last month. Her hair is greying from the temples even though she's still pretty young, had me in a panic in her early twenties after she learnt that she and everyone else in her generation wouldn't have another chance to be parents. As I open the door she sighs pointedly, and I have to hide my irritation. These days I mostly feel annoyance and guilt towards her. She was joyful in moments when I was younger, when it wasn't just us and it wasn't as hot.

I take one final look at our apartment: the windows painted black from inside, which means you can never quite tell whether it's morning or night; the worn furniture with shredded upholstery from our cat Rufus, who I'd attempted to hug goodbye before he scampered beneath my bed; the hardened, half-eaten bowl of plain congee on the table; the bowl of fruit Mum always makes sure to keep full – her one indulgence besides my train fares, and how most of our weekly allowance is spent. These days, one banana goes for about the same price as a new pair of shoes, but if you know who to haggle with at the markets you can come away with a whole hand of ladyfingers that you can freeze and ration for the year.

I start making my way down the hall when Mum calls out.

'Wait,' she says, and splays both hands out in the air, wriggling all her fingers, which means '10pm'. She does it twice for effect. I nod and jog down the stairs.

I take the tunnel to the station because it's boiling and I can't bear the idea of wearing my OCs (Outdoor Clothes) right now. Better to just stay underground where it's a couple of degrees cooler, although I can already feel my skin prickling and itching, and my fringe sticking to my forehead. The cramps make me sweat more. I almost sneaked one of Mum's painkillers this morning, but she said they're only for emergencies, and when I imagined her alone at home with no one to care for her except Rufus, who I'm sure would take a bite out of us if he had the chance, I couldn't go through with it. Instead I sat on the toilet with the lid down and the shower running so Mum couldn't hear me groaning in pain.

On the train, I open the flask of herb soup and take small sips. These days, I can periodically feel my saliva becoming thick and mucousy for no apparent reason; even the smell of rice is too much. I think back to two months ago, when I started throwing up and Mum wordlessly began collecting different herbs from jars she kept in her room. She'd served me up a bowl of soup and rested her hand on my shoulder, stoic, but tapping her foot, which is something she does when she's panicked. 'It might not keep,' I'd said, tears in my eyes. 'A lot of the time they don't keep.' She just sighed and went back to the stove.

There's a young man on the train about three rows ahead of me eating from a steel lunch box; he's pulled the layers out and spread them across his row of seats like a bento. For the first time I'm glad I can't stomach anything because if I had any appetite I'd probably knock him out for a taste of what he's eating. There's rice, marinated pork with brown onions and scallions (I can't remember the last time I ate real meat), some wilted greens, and kim chi. The greens look like spinach. Fresh spinach. I'm guessing he's a maintenance worker, doing one of the riskier jobs that pay tons. For one thing, he's chubby, well fed. He's also got a nice haircut and sparkly stud earrings peeking out from under his black hair. Most guys have buzz cuts, but his hair is properly styled so he looks like one of those Korean pop stars I've seen in archival videos. And nobody travels to the Old City besides maintenance workers and students, most of whom are poor, like me, although Mum and I are certainly not the poorest. He must be one of the electricians or plumbers or cleaners who manage the school buildings to prevent any more big lawsuits happening. One year, before they started hiring workers, a mouldy ceiling collapsed on one student's head. She didn't die, but she got a concussion that led to her developing amnesia, and her parents sued the State government for millions and won … back when you could sue Officials. Another year, a student got electrocuted in a flooded basement because of damaged wiring. He *did* die.

The man is slurping his kim chi now, chewing so loudly and with his mouth wide open, so the pong of garlic and chili, which I normally love, wafts from his big, stubbly mouth into the rest of the carriage. I take more small sips of my soup. Besides the kim chi pong, I'm getting motion sickness from travelling backwards. Mum said when she was growing up the train seats had a mechanism where you could switch the direction of the seats, which I thought was neat, but the levers are all rusted through now, have been for decades.

To distract myself from my stomach, I focus on what the man's focusing on: the passing landscape. There's not much to see through the tinted windows – empty office buildings smattered with bird droppings, weaving motorways dotted with a couple of stationary cars, and lots of ibises. They're perched everywhere: on streetlights that lost their power long ago, without which you can't see much in the evenings unless there's a full moon, and on abandoned luxury cars reflecting the morning glare off their smashed-up windscreens. They stalk down the roads inspecting old food wrappers in that hunched, bobbing motion that makes them look like ancient apothecaries, which I had to play in *Romeo and Juliet* last term because everyone else 'would rather die than play a doctor'. I don't mind the ibises like other people do. At school (the building used to be this big-shot library) I read in this book called *The Definitive Australian Bird Guide* that ibises are native birds. Now they're just about the only ones left, and have started reclaiming the land.

There's a buzzing sound and the man whips out a phone. It's a bit smaller than the other heat-resistant bricks you see around (he's definitely rich) but it still has that keyboard with protruding buttons that make annoying clicking noises as you type. He's got a message, which he reads and thinks about before typing out a response and sending it. *What an idiot,* I think to myself. Sure, he's rich enough to have pork and spinach and the best technology, but I guess wealth and cleverness aren't mutually exclusive. It's not like they tell us that they're watching, that they're monitoring our every move – if they told us that there'd be more rioting than there already is. The control is unspoken, but you see it in the evening smoke rising from people's gardens or balconies (the messages they've written in their notepads that they must burn every night). You see it in the Officials silencing community leaders with emotional blackmail because they know the sexual stuff they've been watching online (the guys in class said they're apparently pornos of white women dressed as farm animals getting done up the butt because it's the only way community leaders can feel some semblance of control anymore, although none of the guys have admitted to watching the videos themselves). And you see it in the demand for Auslan literacy when applying for any kind of job, even at the markets. Actually, *especially* at the markets.

Okay, the man is donning his OCs now and I would thank God aloud if I believed in Him or Her and I wasn't burping up more bile. He packs his lunch box up and pushes sunglasses onto his face and makes his way towards the doors. He passes several people on the platform, about four or five men and women of colour, since it's peak hour and the factories are opening up for the day. There's also a white person – a kid, I'm guessing, from their height – trying to fit their arm into an ancient vending machine to grab a packet of chips, more out of boredom than anything; those chips are probably older than the kid and eating them would probably mean a trip to the doctor's and you'd rather try your luck dying at home than getting any real treatment. Mum says doctors used to be some of the most trustworthy and respected people before every diagnosis and every secret that patients shared with them became the government's business.

A couple of commuters watch the kid, mildly interested, but the others just stare ahead at nothing in particular while fanning themselves, too hot to be present. The kid's got scrappy OCs, probably the descendant of one of the few white workers whose families stood with ours during the first riot and lost their positions as a result. Once the water started rising, everyone wanted to escape the Old City, but there wasn't enough space in the west for us all. I start layering on my OCs, which are in good nick and better quality than most OCs you buy in a store or market, considering Mum had to sew extensions on as I grew. I slip on my long-sleeved shirt; trousers, which get tucked into my socks; a breathable balaclava; polarised sunglasses, and a wide-brimmed hat. I'm already sweating through the shirt, but it's nice to have something tight against my stomach; it eases the cramping.

We're moving into the heart of the Old City now – the end of the line. I can see the heat rising off the bitumen on the platform outside, and the gulls and ibises circling above the water, dried mud caked on their wings. For most of my life, I thought that seagulls and ibises were brown; Mum says the smart birds learnt to cover themselves with mud decades ago to protect themselves against UV rays, while the dumb ones are burnt and covered in cancerous growths or dead and eaten by their comrades or very desperate homeless folk. In the distance, I can make out the Opera House with its arched tips bent sideways like stretching dancers. Mum's told me about the shows she saw there as a child, how there were concerts and ballets and comedies before they shut the place down. There was even an ad for the Melbourne Cup projected onto the Opera House once, when Mum was growing up. Apparently the race caused a big uproar each year because the horses got abused, but I sort of wonder what would have been worse: the horses being shot after injuries then or the horses being boiled alive by the heat today?

The Opera House is boarded up now, but the rumour is that squatters have made nests in the balconies in the old concert hall, where they're high off the ground, far from the water and the mosquitoes breeding in it. If you can tolerate the damp and the cyclonic cold fronts that burst through the broken windows during winter, I can imagine the place making a classy home. You'd have plenty of space and you'd never get bored, unlike the one-bedroom apartments most of us in the New City can afford.

I step off the train and into the open air, where the heat washes over me and makes it difficult to breathe. I take two steps at a time down the dead escalators. At the bottom, my shoes make a giant splash in the water because I forgot to make the extra leap onto the bridging plank to school.

'Shit,' I say aloud, although I never really swear (Mum's only ever had two rules and they're 'Don't swear unless you have to' and … and the other rule I broke), but it's fine because as always I'm the only person at the station. The only other noises around are the squawking birds and the grinding of the ferry bows against shop windows, like nails on a chalkboard, except deeper and sadder, almost a moan. When the ports flooded Circular Quay the ferries rose with the water and now their rusted, empty carcasses bob around the harbour aimlessly.

I'm desperate to get into the air conditioning at school. It's the last time we can feasibly be outdoors before summer; if heat exhaustion doesn't get you, dehydration will. Last year, when fewer people started coming to class because it was just too far out and their parents wanted to save their train fares for rations, I started skipping some classes and breaking into the library stacks, which we were technically banned from entering, but it was so dark and cool and untouched in there I couldn't resist. I found a drawer full of catalogued news articles that said there wouldn't be any cataclysmic disaster that would make the world unlivable for most of the human and animal population; the temperature would simply rise to a point where the climate was hotter than our bodies, which meant that we'd no longer be able to perspire, which meant that we'd slowly start to cook from the inside out. Frog in a pot kind of thing.

'When I read those articles in the paper I fell into a deep depression,' says my mum whenever I grill her about why she had me if she knew what lay ahead. 'I felt like I'd been so irresponsible choosing to have you.' That made me angry, her self-indulgence, because it meant that I couldn't be sad for myself. I just wanted her to say that she wanted me so badly she risked everything to have me.

After every conversation like this Mum looks at me, aghast, and says, 'I'm sorry.' Once, I asked her to clarify why and she said, 'I feel sorry for you,' and didn't stop crying to the point where I had to hug her and that made her cry harder. The only other time she cries is when she talks about my dad, her boyfriend who got king-hit by an Official while protesting, when I was a toddler. Apparently Dad was funny and had small eyes, like me. Mum says he liked to break rules.

Knowing that about Dad inspired me to break into the library. And it was actually there where Raymond and I always hooked up. I had liked him since the first day of school, when we were about twelve years old and he told the teacher he was only studying out of obligation.

'My parents don't even speak Mandarin but they're so desperate to be able to control one thing in their lives they're sending me here to "preserve our culture" because they "don't want me to lose myself like they have,"' he'd said, not bitterly, but matter-of-factly, like that was that, and could we please get on with the lesson now. I didn't have a crush on him then; I just admired that he could speak like that – freely, without fear that the room might be bugged or something. I hadn't seen anyone, let alone another kid, have that much self-respect in public. I remember there being a suspended silence after he spoke, like the class and teacher half expected Officials to break through the ceiling and shoot Raymond dead. It was scary. After that, I avoided him most of the time. It wasn't until maybe two years ago that I started finding those qualities about him attractive. I also liked how he'd furrow his eyebrows when he was trying to get the strokes for a character in the right order; how he'd pack his own lunch, which was normally preserved fruit and congee with a sprinkling of salted peanuts that he kept in a giant container in his desk, and how he'd run his hands through his black, dead-straight hair when he was tired to wake himself up. His pants were also too tight because his parents couldn't afford to buy him new ones – so I understood that he was frugal *and* had a good butt.

'Can I sit here?' I said to him out of the blue one day, around last year. It took him by surprise; his dark eyes flickered from the whiteboard to mine. He always had hard eyes but in that moment of surprise I saw something shift – just a glimmer of softness. Being that close to him, I realised that I'd only ever seen him in profile before, from the safety of my desk – a strong, slightly stubbly jaw line pointed towards the teacher. Now I saw that he had a small, black freckle on his upper lip. His tanned skin was remarkably clear except for a trail of medium-sized pockmarks on his right cheek. When he spoke, I saw that his teeth were white and straight except for one of his front teeth, which curved slightly inwards. I liked these things about him the most, these imperfections that undercut yet somehow defined his handsomeness. I wondered what he thought staring back at me. That I had small, determined eyes, probably, but also that they suited me. That I was bony, with uneven bangs and a shoulder-length bob that I learnt to cut myself, and full lips hiding a chipped incisor from when I was so hungry as a child I tried eating gravel. I wondered if he ever watched me from across the room too. It wasn't that we weren't friendly to each other; we just rarely spoke unless it was part of a group assignment. I gestured to the desk beside him, which was ballsy on my part because the classroom was mostly empty these days, even on those days our teacher bothered to come.

'Sure,' he said, and then we learnt everything about each other through our words: him writing in his notebook and burning the evidence at night, and me scribbling away on my plastic packaging. I learnt that he had two younger sisters, and an older brother who had died of an asthma attack as a baby because of the dust storms. His great-great-grandparents on his dad's side moved to Sydney from Beijing and started a convenience store business which went bankrupt when his dad was a kid and now his parents worked in factories making OCs, which was ironic because they earned so little they couldn't even afford to buy the clothes they were making, had to get by on hand-me-downs from people in the community. Raymond's favourite food was salted eggs, which was something he only ever got on his birthdays. His skin always smelt of salt – probably sweat – but never of BO. And he had a Mongolian spot on his right butt cheek (he flashed me one day when a teacher had their back to us) which never disappeared, even as he grew up. He loved fart jokes and used to have a massive crush on Cherrie, who's Eurasian, before his dad told him that her dad was a cruel and lousy gweilo – he was always cheating on his wife and he punished the workers with lower wages if they took bathroom breaks, so a couple of women had pissed themselves on the job. After Raymond's dad got sick with cancer he shat himself during a twelve-hour shift and had to walk home in his shit-filled pants.

I told Raymond about how my mum was born in Australia to older parents who ran a chain of Chinese restaurants across Sydney. I told him about how my gung gung and po po died from heat stroke when they stayed outdoors for too long trying to protect their restaurants from looters, and how after that Mum fell into a deep depression that only lifted when she met Dad (an international student from Singapore who teased her for only being able to speak English) and then returned after his death. I told him that besides Yu, my best friend was Rufus, who was not affectionate with me but once sat in the lap of another tenant in our building, which infuriated me, and that made Raymond laugh. I told him that for money Mum took on sewing jobs and sometimes travelled to the houses of Officials to do their wives' or mistresses' nails, and that if it weren't for the extra food Mum stole from their pantries – tea leaves, bread and pickles – sometimes we just wouldn't eat for a day. He learnt that my favourite food is ice cubes, which Mum and I get as a treat once a year from the only shop that has a generator large enough to power freezers. And that I have an ingrown toenail that formed when I had a growth spurt and had to wear the same, tight boots for six months until we could afford fabric for Mum to alter them.

One day Raymond found me in the library watching *Alien* for the billionth time, which I do when teachers don't turn up. He silently waited beside me until I stood and led him to the stacks and touched his cheek softly. Then we were kissing and pulling up each other's tops and I turned the volume up on the movie so no one could hear us as he hitched up my skirt, and that time, and all the other times, and just now when I accidentally stepped into the puddle near the station, are the only instances where I've sworn in my life.

'He can't keep a secret,' my mum had written when we figured out a plan. 'Don't you love him?'

I nodded. That's why I broke up with him.

'Then don't make him look guilty too,' she wrote, then erased, and then turned back to the congee on the stove.

'Mum,' I said, and she shot me a warning look, which was fine, but then a desperately sad look that seemed to contain the weight of everything she wanted to tell me and soothe me with. I suddenly felt angry because it hit me that I rarely got to hear her voice, which was warm and comforting, and what I deserve. The most I ever got to hear her speak was when she sang low, lovelorn Mandarin ballads she learnt from her grandmother that neither of us understands, except I've been deciphering the lyrics over the years. Some of them go, *'Do you remember the long lane where we used to walk? Now only touched by the light of the lonely crescent moon ... How could I forget, how could I ever forget? How could I forget the end of spring?'*

I don't even make it to the school building before I see Raymond, Yu and Cherrie sitting inside the convenience store around the corner from school, their faded second-hand OCs balled up by their feet, except Cherrie's, which are brand new and folded on her lap. You could spot Cherrie's pale, pointy face – she bleaches her skin, not that she needs to with the level of sun protection her OCs afford – and bright lipstick from a mile away. Our teacher must have forgotten to turn up again, or she's just done caring, or she can't afford to travel into the Old City anymore, or she's being held in detention somewhere by an Official for something she's said. Teachers are supposed to be impartial – they get in trouble for veering from the curriculum in the tiniest way. Last year a teacher disappeared when he brought an ancient tin of lychees to class. It was an heirloom left by his sister, who had been shot dead by a humiliated Official after she dumped him. We got to share the lychees with him on the anniversary of her death. He didn't tell us any of this, we were just happy to taste something new for the first time and a bit weirded out that he cried for most of the class, but it all came out when he didn't arrive at school the next day. Teachers can disappear for any reason. We've been through dozens of them since we started at school, so we've learnt not to get attached early on.

I enter the shop and pay for a chicken-flavoured instant noodle cup. Even though the flavours in the powder are more artificial than Cherrie the noodles taste homey and the idea of eating them doesn't make me feel nauseous. Yu and Cherrie are deep in a conversation, signing to each other excitedly. Cherrie's pretty up herself about being able to sign because her family has the money to fork out for Auslan classes, but Yu's grounded and only knows how to sign because her brother is deaf, so I'll get the goss about their conversation from her later. They don't see me, but Raymond does, and then pretends like he hasn't. I make my noodles at the self-serve station, which is just a hot water tap and some forks, and bring it over to the small table where they're sitting, by a blacked-out window.

'Hey guys,' I say, and take the seat beside Raymond. He bristles, but not angrily, more out of nervousness.

'Another fruitful day of learning,' says Cherrie, brimming with sarcasm.

'What's the point of coming all the way here if she's not even going to show up?' says Raymond, and I half-wonder whether he should have written that instead of spoken it, but at this point I'm too tired to care. I slept fourteen hours last night and I still feel lethargic. I wonder if I can really withstand months more of this feeling.

Classes have always taken place in the Old City, which was largely abandoned after sea levels rose higher and faster than anyone predicted, or believed would happen, sending most people inland and to the west, to the New City. Besides some graffiti, most of the buildings in the Old City are remarkably intact, just empty. The Queen Victoria building is still regal-looking, even with all the smashed windows and the 'WHITES GO HOME' graffiti scrawled across the statue outside. And the Sydney Tower still rotates sometimes during cyclones – the words 'FUCK OFF' turn round and round in the sky since someone spray-painted them on the glass. If it weren't for the odour, people would probably have stayed, but few can stand the smell of reeking, rotting fish and ibis shit, which coats almost everything. The rent is cheaper here, which means that most of the language schools are here. Typical ethnics.

'Ray,' says Yu, warningly. She drinks the rest of her broth. Hers is seafood-flavoured. 'You know it's not that simple.'

'I'm going to quit classes,' says Ray. 'My parents need the money.' He makes sure not to look at Cherrie when he says this. Cherrie is not our friend – most people have been flung together in class due to a sheer lack of numbers. We're the last generation of 'native settlers' in the country, whatever that means, and so we have to stick together before the first intake of refugees, or so the Officials say.

'Then quit,' says Cherrie. 'What's keeping you here?' She raises her eyebrows at Raymond and me pointedly and sips on her drink, some passionfruit-flavoured thing. Of course none of us have ever tasted passionfruit in real life (most fresh food is shipped in for rich folk from the one plant bank that survived the Svalbard floods). Then Cherrie turns to Yu and clamps her nose shut with her thumb and forefinger. 'Why do you always get seafood flavour? Air not fishy enough for you already?'

'We can't eat any of those fish,' says Yu, teasingly. She burps in Cherrie's face and Cherrie waves the burp away, disgusted. 'Aren't you curious about what tuna tasted like?'

'No. Tuna was full of mercury, anyway,' says Cherrie. Then she gently unfolds her OCs and starts getting dressed.

'Where are you going?' I ask, slurping down my noodles. They're good. I realise that I'm hungry.

'For a walk,' says Cherrie, tetchy. She glances at the three of us, aware that she's on the outer, and leaves. Anyone else, I would have warned. Who goes for walks outside in the daytime? For leisure? But Cherrie wears the top range of OCs, thanks to her parents, and is more protected outside than any high-ranking official. With Cherrie gone, Raymond seems to relax and even manages a smile with me.

'How have you been?' he asks.

'I'm okay. How's your dad?'

He shrugs, which means not good; the past couple of months his dad's been coughing up blood. He takes a swig of my noodle soup and sets the cup back down. He clears his throat.

'I miss you,' he says.

'It's only been two weeks.'

'I know, but you didn't come to class last week and I was worried. Are you feeling better?'

Yu stands up to bin her empty noodle cup and makes a show of browsing the shelves so Raymond and I can be alone.

'Yeah. Just a bug.'

'Dad thought it was just a bug,' he says.

'Let's change the subject,' I say cheerily, my voice strained. I wave Yu over and she returns with a basket full of snacks: barley sugar, water crackers, and salty plums. I'm tempted to ask for some crackers, I'm still hungry, but I know the food is meant to last her for a while.

'What were you and Cherrie talking about?' I ask.

Yu immediately whips out her notepad and scrawls madly, then shoves the paper into my face: 'SHE'S DATING

A DOCTOR.' My stomach sinks. I read the next line: 'Bragging about knowing top secret shit. GROSS.' 'Gross' is underlined twice.

There was a girl named Jasmine in our class who fainted last year. We all thought it was because of heat stroke. She was taken to a doctor to be monitored and when she woke up they'd taken her baby out of her while she was unconscious. They sent her home with two whopping fines: one, for concealment, and another, for not seeking an abortion. Then they brought her to the centre of the New City and made an example of her, kicking her in the stomach repeatedly so it would never happen again. Her family couldn't pay the fines so they were evicted from their home. Jasmine stopped coming to classes, and nobody knew where she or her family went after that. Most people suspected they died from starvation.

When Yu goes to pay for her snacks, Raymond reaches for my hand. I let him hold it. His hands are large and broad, the skin of his palms coarse with calluses from the extra factory work his dad brings home with him. I intertwine my fingers through his and he squeezes my fingers tight in response. My voice catches in my throat. We sit together in silence for some moments.

'Today was going to be my last class,' I say, finally. His attention snaps to me.

'Why?' he asks. I pull my hand away from his and he looks at me, wide-eyed. 'Where are you going?'

For a split second I want to tell him everything. I don't care about my mum or Rufus, or being detained, or losing our apartment and starving to death. I wish that I could be with Raymond, and that our lives could be simple, and the days could be warm, but that the nights would be cool, and that we could have nourishing food, and that we could swim in open water, and eat fresh fruit and vegetables, and that I could have had the opportunity to make my own choices, even if they were mistakes, because they would have been my mistakes, and mine to make.

'I got a job at the market,' I say. He grimaces, knows it's a lie.

'At which stall?' He takes my hand again, gently this time. I want desperately to hug him, to feel his broad, solid chest against my body, to smell his skin and taste its saltiness. I hope the kid looks like him.

White
Flu

Omar Sakr

When all the white people started dying, my cousin Bilal sent me a text saying 'Allahu Akbar!' This was not unusual. The text I mean, not the flu that swept through the colonies and the European heartland. If Bilal didn't declare the greatness of God at least once a week, as he stuffed a leaking Big Mac into his hairy mouth or puffed on a joint or had his dick sucked by a twink, I would have been alarmed. It was the early days of the sickness, and I was sitting by Mum's deathbed in Liverpool Hospital, where I was born. I wondered if they had that bed still, and why people didn't talk about birthbeds with the same kind of recognition or awe as its opposite. I put my phone away, but not quickly enough. Mum's eyes were open now and full of spite.

'Christ,' she said in a cracked, thin voice. 'You won't even let me die in peace.' Her trademark barb lacked force. Her voice had once been a thing of legend, enough to make men cower, and her children freeze streets away. It might have been the setting or my memory playing tricks, but she just sounded old.

'Yeah, it's good to see you too,' I said, shifting on the hard plastic chair. I'd been there only for an hour, trying to take in all the ways she had changed since last I saw her, and failing. Her face was still a stark mask of bronze, sharp cheekbones with a proud nose, but she had shrunk in size, and I could see her skull where her long black hair had thinned out either from age or decades of the acidic spray she would pour on it in the mornings. Her breasts, a gift from her third or fourth husband, looked ridiculously oversized, even within the ill-fitting hospital gown. She looked like a sick child playing dress-ups. I couldn't think of a crueller fate for a woman whose life revolved around her beauty, and I thanked God she was not awake to see my reaction when I walked in. I was certain of one thing: she could survive anything except pity.

'Who told you I was here?' she said, picking fitfully at her blanket.

'Kholto,' I said. Her sister, her rival. There was no need to specify which aunty, there was only one that either of us spoke to – Rania, or the Virgin Mary as Mum called her. Rania had six kids, of course – every Arab woman was taught to act as if the world was ending and only she could repopulate it, which speaks either to a deep intelligence or deep trauma or both, because the Arab world was forever ending and now it seemed the rest of the world was too – but Mum said she still acted like she'd never seen a dick, she was such a pious prude.

'What did she say? Is she coming?' She was carefully looking away, staring fixedly at the small flatscreen TV above her head. I wasn't meant to hear the hope in her voice, but it burrowed under my skin. Shame burned in my blood. No one should be reduced to hope. Unsure of what to say, I looked up too, at a flicker of red. 'Breaking News: Killer Flu Toll Rises' scrolled across the bottom of the screen. A concerned white woman appeared, her hair a blonde curtain. You could tell she was concerned because there was a single perfect furrow above her eyebrows, and her voice was low and serious. In a minute they would cross to a stunned family, a pale hand holding a grim microphone up to chapped lips, then they would cross back to the studio where the white woman would be joined by a doctor who would tell people to get their shots, that flu season was serious, that it was bad this year but they were handling it. It had been like this all month, all my life. Concern and reassurance, the most powerful drugs invented, doled out in slices every day.

'She said you were here, and that I should check on you,' I said. As her eyes flashed with disappointment I quickly added, 'But I'm sure she'll come see you, too. She will.' I didn't say that I almost hadn't come either, that the years of silence after I was outed as bisexual had been the best years of my life and I wasn't eager for them to end.

'Yeah right,' Mum snorted. 'That one never does anything that doesn't benefit her. Turn this khara off, would you.' She gestured at the TV as if she were still my mother and I still her child, and I silenced the white woman.

'Bro, straight out, it's a conspiracy,' Bilal said as he crunched on cornflakes. We were sitting in his mum's garage, which was kitted out with a patchy leather couch, big TV, and a rotting punching bag. The roller door had not been opened in ages, and the place smelled like a mixture of unwashed animals and pot.

'I thought you said it was Allah taking out the "infidels"?'

'What? No man, keep up.' He paused for a second, milk outlining his stubbled mouth. 'It's the Jews.'

'But they're dying too,' I said. It was true: my Jewish housemate had texted me just the other night to say his aunty had gotten the 'white flu', and died within days. It had started as a joke online, calling it that, despite the TV doctors saying there was no way to know for sure at this stage. It quickly became understood that it was devastating the West in particular, and people of European or Anglo descent seemed to be the only ones dying. Ancestry dot com crashed and kept crashing from the demand: everyone suddenly wanted to know where they came from. My housemate's family were thinking of fleeing to Asia or Africa to get away from other whites. The problem, he confided, was that white people were already doing that in droves of pinkish panic, and the authorities in those countries were starting to crack down. Airports were being closed and cordoned off into quarantined areas.

'That's what they want you to think. It's 9/11 all over again.' Bilal slurped at the dregs in his bowl, and put it down with a wet sigh.

I considered that for a minute, my head still fogged from the last hit of the bong, and Bilal crowed with triumph. 'See, see! Even you, you liberal Jew-lover, you can't deny it.' He relaxed back on the couch, spreading his thick legs until his paint-flecked work pants rubbed up against my jeans.

I laughed because it was easier to laugh than to do the work of fighting an idiot. Bilal, like most of the family, didn't finish high school. I was the only one who went to university and the running joke was that I had never come back, that I was still there instead of in 'the real world' like the rest of them. I looked from Bilal's thigh up to his face: he was watching me, smirking. No one that ugly should be so confident, I thought. His face was too wide, his nose too fat, and he was built like a forward. He had the loveliest eyelashes in the world though, long and dark and thick. I could never dismiss him totally because he'd been smart enough to know me before I knew myself. It was Bilal who took me aside one Eid, in the back of Kholto Linda's yard, as hundreds of rellos milled around the tables of food, and hissed in my ear, 'I know what you are, bro. It's okay, I'm gay too.'

Then he laughed a garlic laugh in my face and stumbled off.

Later, when I told him I was bi, he just shrugged and said, 'Whatever, same shit. You're still a cocksucker.' He was right, and I proved it on him. We only did it the once but it was seared into my mind, in part because it had been here on this couch that I went down on his long cut dick, and because it was my first. Bilal's hand was sneaking up to his crotch. We were both there, in that moment, in the silent unconscious way two people can travel into the same memory. Our bodies were reacting to the past, hardening as the early tension before sex tightened the air. Then his phone rang, lighting up in the dank dimness of the garage, and he grimaced before answering it.

'Bill,' he said, then listened to the brash bogan voice on the other end for a minute before saying 'Right now?' and 'Yeah, I'll be there.' He was on his feet, readjusting himself in an obvious way. 'Stay if you want,' he said, too casually. I nodded but I would be out of there as soon as he was gone, and he knew it too.

My aunty Rania was not a famous beauty, nor did she have a voice of legend, she was small and round and soft-spoken. Her weapon of choice was guilt, but she was also deadly accurate with her open-toe shahayta, the cracked backs of which I was staring at as she stood on a step ladder and picked at the vine leaves growing in her backyard. The midday sun hit her hijab, the stunted lemon tree, the grass, and the wood latticework around which the dark green vines twisted and twirled; I had to squint as I looked up at her and listened to her complain about her aching arms, her useless children who weren't there to help her, ya Allah where had she gone wrong, and so on. I was looking at her heels, which were as cracked as the soles of her shoes, and thinking about how often I'd had to dodge the thrown missiles, how I was never fast enough, and how funny it was, the ease with which violence can become a game. I was seized by an urge to kiss her feet. I managed to resist, but it was a near thing.

'What are you looking at, you stupid boy?' The fact she had been silent for a full minute registered at the same time as her words, her pet phrase for me, which took a moment to absorb. I knew I was taking too long to answer. Rania's smooth oval face was concerned within her brown hood, lips pursed; she looked like an owl, pensive and predatory.

'Nothing,' I said finally. 'What were you looking at?' She had been staring over the neighbour's fence. Probably snooping to see if Frank had come down with the flu and carked it in his yard. When I had played with my cousins out here and we'd accidentally kicked the footy or soccer ball over the fence, Frank would take a kitchen knife to it, his fair skin going red right to the tips of his grey hair, before sending the mutilated rubber back to us. What a kalb. For the first time, I felt something eager and hot in my chest at the thought that he might die, and the flu became real.

'Nothing,' she snapped. 'Stop distracting me, I don't have all day.'

'Do you want help?' I said, aware already that she would say no.

'Like you know what to do.' She sniffed, and kept snipping at the vines, putting the leaves into the bag tied to her hips. 'This was Teyta's favourite, you know. She taught me.' My grandmother, Allah yerhama, had stood where my aunty stood, and picked the vines in just the same way and let loose the same complaints. She didn't have a tree of her own, her and Jido had lived in the flats in Warwick Farm, so she would come here when the season was right to prepare the dish it was meant for, warra eynab. I used to adore watching her sit on the floor inside, a sheet spread out before her, as she rolled rice into each green palm. Squinting in the bright light, Aunty Rania could almost have been her, which is what she wanted more than anything. Maybe we all secretly want to be our mothers. It would explain why I was such a fuck-up, at least.

'I saw Mum the other day,' I said.

She didn't reply for a minute, then, 'How was she?'

I thought of Mum lying in that bed like crumpled sandpaper, and said, 'Humdulilah. She woke up for a bit, and was swearing at me within ten minutes.'

Aunty Rania laughed and her whole body shook with it, delight making her beautiful, before it turned into a raspy smoker's cough. 'You'll kill me, you stupid boy,' she said, but she was smiling as she moved onto a new section of the vines.

'You need to stop smoking, Kholto.' I'd said it a hundred times and knew what was coming: a sigh, followed by, 'We've all gotta go some day and only Allah knows when and how.' I knew she believed it, and I also knew it had nothing to do with her inability to quit smoking, or why she chose to say it so often to me. The script was familiar and easy for both of us, a way out of the silence that threatens to fall between any two people who spend time together, a way out from asking or answering hard questions, like, 'Will you visit your sister please?' I don't know how to talk to the woman who birthed me or to you, the woman who raised me, I'm not even sure what's wrong with Mum, what's wrong with us; why can't we be normal?

I masturbated hard and fast to the idea of being fucked by my ugly cousin, coming quickly. I wiped away the white remains, and lay for a moment in the afterglow of shame. It was okay so long as it remained in my head, and that one teenage transgression surely didn't count. It was dark in my room and my housemate was out. My nipples were hard. Desire still pulsed through my body, restless, unrelieved. I went into the bathroom naked, wanting to get a selfie before my dick shrank to its normal size. I took it with practised ease, my short body angled to hide the soft swell of my belly, highlighting the curve of my arse. I opened Grindr; it was old-fashioned, and largely seen as the province of creeps and sex fiends, but it's what I grew up on. After checking the last dozen ignored 'hey' messages, I sent the selfie to the top six. It didn't really matter who was behind the profiles, I only interacted with those that had a headless torso as the photo, or a blank square – they were most often brown or black men, or else older whites and religious types who still lived under shame's foot. Thank God. They would want to ruin me in secret, and only I would get to see the moment they cracked open, the widening of their eyes, the heaving of their sweat-slicked hairy chests as they gave in to what ruled them.

My phone lit up. I stared in disbelief at the caller ID, 'Brother,' my skin going cold. Arousal vanished. My brother had outed me to the family and, later, stood outside my room watching as I packed my bags, like he was already planning where to put his dumbbells. We had never been close. He was a bully, I was a bitch, and our mum didn't give a shit. My hand shook. I thought about letting it go to voicemail; I thought about Mum, dead. I answered.

'Yeah?' I said. Tried to anyway, my throat was so tight and dry. I cleared it and had to repeat myself.

'Jamal,' he said, and I closed my eyes at the familiar timbre of his voice saying my name, the surge of fear and loss. 'Look, I don't want to be doing this any more than you, but things are fucked right now.'

'Yeah,' I said.

'I'm worried about Amelia, bro. And the kids, with this flu thing. You know about this shit, with all your books and that. What should we do?'

'Uh …' I had to think for a moment to place the name. He was referring to his white wife. Bilal had told me about her – she was a dentist or something – back when they had the wedding I had not been invited to attend. Bilal was still closeted, safe in his big blokey masculinity, and for the first few years he'd been my main lifeline to the family, at least until Aunty Rania came around.

'I thought you were calling about Mum,' I said, and heard him suck in a breath.

'What about her? I don't talk to her anymore, she's a disaster.'

'She's in the hospital, didn't anyone tell you?' I said.

'I don't talk to anyone anymore,' he said, and I could hear that he was agitated. 'What about this flu, *bro*?' I realised then that he was terrified. My brother, my tormentor. The man who had relentlessly drilled into my head that I was a useless sissy, too weak for footy, too soft for real work, and who would not hesitate to wade into a knife fight, was scared enough to ask me for help. I couldn't believe it. I scrambled for something to say, something that would reassure him; there had been many epidemic scares over the past decade or so, swine flu for one, bird flu, Ebola, the Zika virus, Zika One, and they all ended up being contained, the cost hidden away, the devastation unrecorded unless one or two patients ended up in America or Australia or the UK. Then there would be hysteria for a while, and the spectacle would go on for days. None of that would mean anything to him.

'It's probably a hoax, bro,' I said. 'There's always a flu season, and people always die. I read somewhere that all sorts are getting it, and it isn't always fatal. Anyway, I wouldn't worry about it.'

'Yeah?' he said, like he desperately wanted to believe me, then softer, 'Yeah. You're right, I thought that too you know, you can't trust these Jews, but I wasn't sure.' We talked for a minute after that. His wife wasn't sick but her throat had been ticklish today, and the kids, three little Arab Anglos, well they were always getting sick. But they would be fine, right? They had to be.

After the call I went back to my room feeling vaguely sullied. How much could one be expected to forgive? In the face of catastrophe, the world appeared to be saying 'everything'. I crawled into bed resentful. It seemed right to ignore the notifications on my phone, to leave the men I had stirred, wanting. It was one of those nights where no one got to be happy.

I stared at the unfamiliar brown news anchor on the TV, then around at the hospital lobby and corridors where dark women in green scrubs were hurrying back and forth – the anchor looked like most of the nurses here, only her face was perfectly made up. It was muted, so I couldn't hear her voice, but I imagined it as a posh British one. I focused again on the captions: 'Australian MP Jack Thrush today repeated the claims of far-right extremists on the internet who believe a white genocide is underway, and that minorities are to blame.' It cut to footage of angry white people on the streets, faces flushed, teeth bared, arms raised – I'd seen this many times before. Was it my imagination or were there more of them than usual? The camera panned and I felt a sick lurch in my gut. There were definitely more, and they weren't all proud Nazis. Many looked like they were on their lunch break from work or were young enough to be students like me. The brown anchor lady's face didn't change once as she repeated their ideas; that they were afraid, that their fear was legitimate, that something had to be done.

I moved on as the topic changed to sports, heading over to the reception desk. I asked after Mum, in case she had been moved or sent home, and was relieved to hear she was still there. Knowing that my brother didn't speak to her made me appreciate just how isolated she was; I didn't realise I had been relying on him to be there for her. If she'd been discharged, I wouldn't even know where to go – last I heard she lived in Villawood, with 'all the junkies and drug dealers', as she had said then, sneering, which was odd because she had been both of those things at one time or another. She still saw herself in her prime, twenty years younger, making men dance to her tune, admired and envied by her sisters, and cursed by her brothers. Maybe she did drugs, maybe she sold drugs, but she was never defined by either. I wish I had that power. As I made my way through the beige hospital corridors, I got a text from my cousin Dina, a gossip who lived in Melbourne; she was across all the family group chats.

—I heard ur mum has AIDS cuz, is it true?

I typed back: who said that?

—Kholo Buktikh

I snorted. We called him Uncle Watermelon because of his big oblong gut, or because of his sloppy smile, depending on our mood when asked. He looked like a jolly bald man, but something had curdled in him young, and he was known to spread cruel rumours.

—U must be desperate if ur listening to him lol

I didn't say anything else. I liked Dina, usually. As a single straight woman who worked in security, she was the next closest thing to a pariah in our family after me and my mum, so we'd kept in touch a bit, but this wasn't something I wanted to spread any further. Besides, I could never admit I didn't know why Mum was sick, and as a queer boy growing up, I heard AIDS flung around as a kind of spectral bogeyman, so of course the thought had occurred to me as well. Even though it was curable now, the stigma of it remained, particularly in our family. It could be one of the reasons Mum was being shifty, and had told the doctors and nurses to stay quiet too. I tried not to think of embarrassing reasons to be hospitalised, because then I would have to think about her body; the more abstract it was, the better. *It's definitely in her butt, bro. Ass cancer for sure.* Bilal's voice. I was trying not to think of him, too.

If all the things I didn't want to think about came into my head, my skull would explode, which just about sums up being Lebanese. No one can repress like we can – it's what makes us dangerous. 'If Lebanon can pretend a civil war didn't happen, we can pretend anything,' my Jido would often say, rubbing the bullet scar on his thin chest. I could never tell if he was proud or sad about that.

'Oh, would you shut the fuck up, you miserable cow.' Mum's hard voice blared out of the room ahead of me and I couldn't help but laugh. When it wasn't aimed at you, it was easy to admire the brutal efficiency of her tongue, how quick she could cut a person to pieces.

'Asalaam wu alaikum,' I said loudly as I walked in. Mum was sitting up in her bed, hair tied back in a bun, chest swollen against her black singlet. She wore faded torn-up blue jeans and her brown feet were arched, toenails painted a hot pink. Her face was made up, her eyes smoky and dark, that singular vitality I'd so missed was back in force, aimed squarely at a middle-aged white woman in the bed next to her. The white woman's jowls sagged in shock. She stammered into the phone held up to her ear, then said, 'I'll have to call you back, love.' She hung up.

'Thank God!' Mum said, turning to me. 'Hi darling.'

I raised my eyebrows as I sat by her bed. I was back to being a darling. She really might be dying. 'Mum, what's going on?'

'Oh, this bitch has been going on and on all morning, I have the flu I do I have it, oh god, boo hoo.' She waved her arms in the air, putting on a shrill mocking tone. 'It's so pathetic. None of these clowns know how to die with any dignity, astugfirullah. Now Arabs, we don't know how to do anything else.'

'I meant with you,' I said.

'Oh. That,' she said, waving a hand airily. 'It's nothing. They're just doing some scans; I'll be out of here in no time.'

I nodded as if I believed her. 'Have they got you on painkillers?'

She sneered. 'Like I'd take anything they offered. I've got better shit in the boot of my car than they have in this whole joint.'

The woman next to her was shooting affronted glances at us, but Mum didn't even notice. 'And what about you?' she said. 'Why haven't I heard from you in all this time?'

I gaped at her and she stared back, defiant. My first visit we hadn't addressed my sexuality or absence at all, it had been too big, too strange and strained. I had hoped it would continue like that, but I should have known better. If there's one thing my mother does best, it's leave me unsettled. They say the way to paradise lies at the feet of your mother. I sometimes wonder if heaven needs better directions. Her hot-pink nails glared at us both until finally something broke, and it wasn't her. It was on me, and it would always be on me, this mountain of obligation. '… I've been busy with uni. I'm sorry, immi.'

Her hard mouth softened. 'Yeah well, don't do it again.' She relaxed back against the bed, suddenly exhausted, face slackening until I could see the tips of her teeth. She was no better than before. Her clothes, her make-up, it was all a front. She'd been expecting me this time. She must have been horrified the other day when I showed up unannounced and saw her as a child should never see their mother: vulnerable, and unable to help herself.

Her eyes fluttered open. 'Are you still ...?'

'Yes,' I said. I tugged the blanket out from under her as she murmured a sleepy protest, then tucked her in. I sat there for over an hour as she slept, remembering the time Teyta, then Jido had been sick, in this same hospital, and the non-stop train of visitors they had, the stacks of plastic containers left by their bedside filled with koosa, kibbe, shourba and loubyeh. It would not do for them to eat terrible Anglo food, they never had, not once since leaving the homeland during the war – they had never even been to a restaurant or café here. Food was home in a way cities or countries could never be, and Mum was nowhere.

To be an El-Hage was to be married to secrets. No one ever said it outright, because it too was a secret; it was something learned by listening and watching. Don't tell the neighbours anything about us, don't tell these particular relatives that we visited the other branch of the family, no your friends can't stay over, what would they say and who would they say it to? Everything had to be rigidly controlled because anything, even a whisper said at the wrong moment, could destroy us. It was the perfect education for a queer boy, or would have been if I wasn't such a faggot. Faggots love secrets, but we also love telling them. It's why we always end up giving ourselves away. My fingers dug into the fake leather of the couch as Bilal fucked me hard, pleasure edged with pain lancing deep into my gut, and I wondered who I would tell about this: how I had rocked up to his garage the afternoon he had off, knelt in front of him and said, 'Break me.' Maybe no one. Maybe this is what I would take to the grave.

We didn't talk after. I had known, walking in there, exactly what to say to get him to act, and I had known too that it would undo our friendship and even our kinship. Every child knows there is power in a destructive act, and sometimes it felt like this was the only power left to me. I went back to the Newtown share house I lived in, a shambling terrace worth more than I would ever earn, and opened the door to emptiness. The furniture was gone. It had all been the property of other people, the detritus of other homes, but somehow I had convinced myself that it was mine by virtue of simply being present.

My room was untouched at least. I checked my phone and saw I had several unread messages, a couple from Dina that I ignored, and one from my housemate that I immediately opened. His family were heading to America, where they would try to get into Mexico. Mexico was busy trying to finish Trump's failed wall, but the border was still as porous as ever. He was sorry, but he had given 'his stuff' to his girlfriend. I considered asking why they hadn't tried regional towns or even the local land councils – didn't they know this country was full of black people? – but truly I didn't care enough, and anyway, Aboriginal people had been through more than enough.

Social media was rife with similar stories, #WhiteLivesMatter, riots of protest and riots of celebration, interspersed with more natural disasters. I turned my phone off. My room didn't feel like my room anymore. I got up, wandered onto the streets, which seemed as full and busy as ever, and after a few hours found myself back at the hospital. It was packed full of worried white people, some looking truly woeful, surgical masks over their faces. Those masks were everywhere now, not just on Chinese imports who were used to breathing smog instead of air. I headed to Mum's room but she wasn't there anymore, a young white man lay in her place. I asked if he knew what happened to the lady before him, but he just shook his snotty head. He'd been crying.

Panic was imprinted on every face I saw, and I was beginning to feel it too. I took off, heading to Aunty Rania's. No one was answering my calls. Outside my aunt's house in Lurnea, there were half a dozen cars. Something had happened, for sure. I was walking through water, an ocean between here and there. I had to drag my heavy legs forward onto the verandah, a roaring noise blanketing my ears. I yanked open the flyscreen door, dripping wet, and stared. There was Aunty Rania, Aunty Hanadi, and Bilal's mum, Aunty Wafat. There was Uncle Buktikh – Brahim to his face – and there was Mum, sick but alive at the table, in front of her favourite meal, warra eynab, the painstakingly rolled vine leaves and lamb on the bone cooked over several days. They were all talking over each other, and the TV was on in the background, as it always was, announcing the end of the world as if it hadn't ended a hundred times for us already, as if we didn't know how to die with dignity.

Black Thoughts

Miscegenation

Hannah Donnelly

I broke my arm in Eugowra, a small place in central New South Wales, in the summer holidays before I started Year 3. I was at my uncle's place with his stepkids. The older kids were going for a paddock bash in an old beat-up car with buckets for seats. Me and my younger cousin wanted to go for a ride on our bikes. I didn't have my own bike, I had my brother's old BMX, the colours of fire sprayed over the black frame. I was ashamed that I didn't have a real bike and had to ride the BMX everywhere like a tomboy. I tried to accessorise with blue handlebar pads but it looked dumb. That day in the paddock me and my cousin were told firmly by my dad and uncle, her stepdad, to stay away from the boys hooning around. We weren't allowed to ride up the long dirt driveway to the main road. Like normal kids, we ignored the rules and rode over to where the boys were doing burnouts.

I'm not sure what instinct alerted me, but I remember looking out across the paddocks to the black asphalt road and seeing Dad and Uncle back from town in the old Ford Falcon. They would be pissed if they saw us riding out here. I screamed at my cousin and we started pedalling back as fast as our eight-year-old legs would take us. There would be no mercy, I knew. I don't remember seeing the pothole. The world lurched and I went face-first over the handlebars. As I landed in the gravel, the bike somersaulted through the air, picking up height and momentum before it crashed down on my elbow. I jumped up and said, 'Shit, I think my elbow is broken.'

My cousin reckoned I would be crying if my elbow was really broken. I got back on the bike and rode to her house. I couldn't move my arm. I tried hard not to focus on the pain. I would be yelled at if I cried, I had to be tough. My uncle's girlfriend gave me a cheese-and-vegemite sandwich: I bit into the salty deliciousness and swallowed my screams.

Dad laughed going over the speed bumps as we drove to Forbes to visit his friend Tim – an angry intellectual who drinks whisky instead of water. He was the only one of Dad's mates from high school I met growing up. I only heard about his other school friends, the ones who committed suicide or overdosed, when Dad was self-medicating. It was at Tim's I watched *The Fifth Element* for the first time. My dad tore up a pillowcase to fashion a makeshift sling while I stared at the TV. It took me out of this world. That's when I started to love science fiction movies. Not all of it is good, though. What's that one where the astronaut on the international space station is wearing the future Australian flag? I think

the actor is Hugo Weaving. No, Eric Bana. Or maybe Sam
Neill. Whatever, same thing. Anyway, he was wearing a
standard white spacesuit with a flag patch on the shoulder.
The Koori flag replaced the Union Jack in the blue sky with
the striking Southern Cross. It still pisses me off that they
imagined our flag in their future. Australia doesn't exist. It
is science fiction already. Our flag in space could only exist
as a symbol of resistance to the colonial settlement of the
multiverse.

We haven't even dealt with the settlement of Wiradjuri
country. How did my self-described poofter Scottish grandpa
end up on a farm in Eugowra in the 70s? A homophobic faith
rejecting his bisexuality, bad divorce and drugs. Grandpa's
farm was in the business of 'pistachio trees' but there was
something else his farm was growing. And my dad was selling. That's how my parents met. My mum followed her crazy
pothead brother through the bush to his business partner,
and it was there she spied on Dad through the trees. Dad was
living on the Lachlan riverbank, homeless, selling drugs and
camouflaging his trail from the cops. I don't know how long
he camped on the river. When my mum became pregnant,
she was just sixteen and her family weren't going to allow this
Aboriginal man to be a father. One of her brothers pulled a
shotgun on my dad and told him to fuck off and never come
back. Mum didn't care what her family thought and ran away

to live with Dad. The sweethearts' first home was a dilapidated weatherboard house on a property out past Yarrabandai with no running water and electricity. That's where my sister was born.

But that's neither here nor there. It was at Grandpa's farm, with my arm swelling up like a beach ball, that my parents fought cause my dad said doctors wouldn't be working on the weekend. They would all be playing golf. It hurt so much that Mum had been feeding me broken-off bits of Dad's codeine tablets so I could get to sleep. Three days later I was taken to the GP. I've never seen a doctor that angry before, or since. He yelled at my parents, 'I should call DOCS!' I held my breath. They'd already taken my older half-brother away. Later, when he calmed down, the doctor said my elbow was a mess, no tendon was left attached to the smashed bones. I was taken to Orange Base Hospital for an emergency elbow reconstruction.

That was one of the best summer holidays I ever had. Grandpa took me to see *Titanic* at the cinemas and I got a cute new shirt with flower buttons to replace the one they had to cut off my body before surgery. And when I started school, I had a cool story to tell. I was a bit disappointed because stitches all the way up my arm meant I didn't get a full cast for everyone in my class to sign. I had this gross clear wound dressing full of dried-up blood, and a half cast. A racist kid named Ben who was known for calling all the black kids smelly boongs pointed at me in the school oval and sneered, 'A half cast for a half caste.'

We are the descendants of the future imaginary messy with blood. Messed up blood that didn't get bred out. A well-versed line of the Australian fantasy is, 'But I'm not responsible for what my ancestors did.' What sickness is this where ancestors wouldn't be thinking of the future and descendants would deny their plans? They say please can't you see it wasn't me who killed and raped and stole? They beg me to understand. Why do you blame white people? They beg me to understand. Why can't you be grateful for the technology we brought? They beg me to understand their innocence, but snarl at me to shut up when I mention the sins of this country, 'Why can't you get over it?'

The true Australia was the white Australia that 'dealt' with the Aboriginal problem. The policies of assimilation were supposed to breed us out. The Chief Protector of Aborigines in Western Australia and the father of biological absorption theory, A.O. Neville, argued that miscegenation could assimilate us. Neville was a pure capitalist white supremacist evil genius. He tested out the model for stations and settlements – in any other reality known as labour camps

– where Aboriginal children would live until they were of an age to be sent off to work as slaves on cattle stations and in rich city mansions.

In my mid-twenties, I was working for an Aboriginal child and family advocacy organisation. We were constantly writing submissions and recommendations about the disturbing rate of Aboriginal kids in out-of-home care. I was doing some research to compare various historical policies of removal to current practices and started reading about Neville's book, *Australia's Coloured Minority* (1947), which documents the breeding-out of colour through photographs of his subjects. His grainy black-and-white headshot popped up with a warty-looking nose. I knew immediately I had uncovered a huge conspiracy.

I believe that Auber Octavius Neville the Chief Protector never died and in fact, if you google any picture of Nev you will come to the same conclusion: he looks too much like a certain conservative political commentator who rose to infamy in the early 2000s. What if they are all still alive, all the protectors of Aborigines, out there writing and broadcasting the superiority of the white race? It's not a huge leap to think those so interested in blood and eugenics would have been partial to a little bit of genetic copying and cloning. It makes sense when you think about it – these clones running the country get so undone by fairskin Aboriginal pride.

Happens nearly every day now. They failed to breed out our Aboriginalness.

In high school, years after he laughed at my half cast, I gave Ben exactly what he deserved. We were lining up for science class and he said in my direction, 'Why do flies always hang around coons?' I choked him out behind our classroom until he cried.

Displaced

Zoya Patel

I remember the waves. The way they used to be. How the edges would ripple like a curtain, gently unfurling on the shore until the foam washed through and left bubbles to glint on the white sand.

It was more grit than sand – the shells still stony and hard, not yet pummelled into a fine grain like the beaches in Australia. In Fiji, the land still felt wild, untamed. The sand told a tale of time, the weathering of the shore.

There are no stories left. It is all ocean now.

The line of people at the immigration centre is long, stretching from the registration counter to the door, and even extending a few people deep outside. I am somewhere in the middle, between an old man who smells strongly of cologne, and a woman with a child, who is swaying from side to side as she waits. The line is a spectrum of colours and voices, ranging from the deep, rich brown of the South Sudanese man at the very front, through the olives and browns of the Pacific, all the way to the woman speaking to her mother in Polish at the back. As different as we are, we are united by our hunger for our turn to plead our case to the officers at each window.

I am fidgeting. I pull my phone out of my pocket, click it open, and then close it again.

The queue moves forward minutely and I shuffle half a step. There is a low murmur of voices in the room, occasionally interrupted by the electronic voice announcing the next number to be served. Despite this system, designed to negate the need to line up, here we stand. I guess queuing makes us feel like we're doing something.

I look around impatiently. The room is grey and green – the colours of the Department of Immigration and Border Enforcement. They changed the name not long ago from Border Protection. With this has come a new set of procedures for those of us seeking residency for ourselves or those we love.

I hate this line but I am grateful to be here rather than there. This is a wait with an end. We don't know how long the wait will be for my family.

At first it was just snippets – the occasional article in the newspaper mentioning rising sea levels, the infrequent conversations between politicians about Australia's role in the Pacific.

I was cocooned, no longer thinking of myself as rooted in the Pacific, even though both of my homes are situated in it.

Fiji felt distant, further than a four-hour flight; a place of memories, of the past. Even the people still there – grandmother, aunties, cousins – felt to me like they belonged in a different dimension, so far removed were they from my life.

I only had the memories, fleeting and fragmented, from my early visits back to the Islands as a child. My grandmother in her worn out kameez, only in her fifties but already bent from working in the sugarcane fields, with her pocket forever full of the chewy strawberry candy that I loved so much.

My cousins, all older than me, playing complicated ball games in the dusty courtyard in front of the family farmhouse. It baffled me, even as a child, to see them so content with their meagre resources – the house old and crooked, inherited when the British left Fiji in the 1970s; the clothes, handed down from one to the other until all siblings had worn them, regardless of gender; the toys, usually made from re-appropriated household items – a broom handle with a rough piece of wood taped to the end becoming a cricket bat, a scrunched-up wad of raffia bags taped into the cricket ball.

I joined in when I was there, but they still felt like strangers to me, our lives just too different. I loved them in the weeks we were together, and forgot them for the months we were apart.

But then the cyclones started. Fijians – both Indian and kaiviti – are no strangers to the storms. The wind that howls with its own voice; the rain that comes in ferocious bursts, falling as though a bucket has been tipped in the sky and the water has descended in one sheet.

When a cyclone is announced, Fijians know the drill. The louvres are closed, belongings brought inside. Food is stocked up, the cooking done before the power cuts out.

Storms are to be weathered, and Fijians have weathered a lot already.

But this was different. Cyclones out of season, coupled with heat that made the roads sticky with melting tar. It felt as though there was an endless amount of damage – buildings lashed by storms then suffering from power outages as the heat caused blackouts across the islands.

The number of villages forced to migrate to higher land went from three or four to sixty, and the convoys of people began to grow, cities bursting at their seams.

I watched from my house in Canberra with a mix of fear and relief. I was an Australian now. I belonged to a different class from my relatives, safe in the First World.

Besides, these were problems but they were not insurmountable. The Fijian Government would create shelters, they would develop housing plans, they would seek aid. They knew this was coming.

When the announcement was made in Australia about the camps, I was sure it couldn't be true. That the old immigration detention centres still existed wasn't surprising – no one had believed it when the Government said they were closed for good – but that they would be filled once again with people from across the ocean was jarring.

'It's temporary,' I told my sister as we watched the news. 'They'll be settled soon. Our family won't need to evacuate anyway, they're safe in Suva.'

The mass departure meant the economy slumped, businesses closing throughout the capital. Soon, the queues for Australian asylum grew, and we watched as, one by one, our relatives joined them.

I was haunted by visions of an abandoned country – islands reverting to a wild and green state. I imagined the lush, wet foliage of Fiji encroaching on pavement, streets sprouting with weeds, vines crawling up the sides of buildings. I imagined the houses empty and looted by the stragglers remaining on the islands. I pictured the resorts, so loved by Australian tourists, subsumed into the wilderness they tried to tame.

On the internet, satellite images showed the water rising, millimetre by millimetre. I wondered how long until the islands would be gone forever. I wondered if you could be Fijian when Fiji didn't exist.

In the queue, I listen idly to the conversations of people around me. With each passing month, the diversity of my fellow seekers increases. At first, we were similar – Fijian-Indian, Pacific Islander, waiting for news of when our families would be released from the camps. But now, the mix is different. I hear snatches of Indonesian, even the French of New Caledonia. It seems like every month there is a new country in crisis. Australia is a reluctant provider. This island continent is not sinking but it is thirsty, and there is not enough to quench the needs of the millions demanding sanctuary. I imagine taking the water that has swallowed my home and pouring it into the cracks of Australia's deserts.

I wish it were that easy. I wish this made sense. Another number is called. We shuffle forward in unison.

When I am not in line, I am at work, mired in the tedium of bureaucracy. The irony is not lost on me that I am working for the very system that imprisons my family. I might not be in the Department of Immigration, I might be working in the more cuddly-sounding portfolio of the Arts, but it is all the same machine. I push paper around my desk each day, policy briefs for projects that feel meaningless in the face of the environmental crisis. It is work, but it feels like a luxury compared to what my family is enduring.

At my desk, I proudly display photos of my grandmother, aunts and the two cousins who languish with them in the camps. I say 'my desk', but this is a fantasy. We all hot-desk now – the culture of the country is impermanence, a lack of ownership, the instruction never to *settle*. We pack our things into little baskets at the end of the day and lock them away in small cupboards.

I travel on the tram to my small apartment, perched tall in a skyscraper along Canberra's central avenue. They built these boxes in the sky and priced them like castles. When I lie in bed, I tower high above the homeless who shelter sometimes under the awnings of the building's façade.

In every movement, every space, I feel the pulsing of my family's hearts tethered to mine by kinship. They are out there, waiting. Their home is swept away and their existence is being slowly eroded by paperwork and officials and emails and fees and errors and endless procedure.

I hate thinking of them locked inside concrete walls when they have lived their lives in a country surrounded by vegetation. My grandmother's property sprawled across acres of green fertile land in Lautoka. The vines under the house crept up over the handrail of the front steps, and the grass was so thick, so soft, it was like carpet.

When we visited, I would run barefoot after my cousins, into the tall forests of sugarcane, unafraid of red-back spiders and brown snakes.

When we saw frogs and lizards, we threw our small heads back and roared with laughter, bounded after them, tried to clutch them with our little fingers. The environment was our home. We did not fear it. We did not tame it.

Sugarcane grew wild, without the orderly rows I see in crops farmed in Australia. We didn't force growth in our bounty, we nurtured it, and celebrated its progress. When we burned the fields after harvest, it was regeneration, not destruction.

Now fires rage across Australia at their own will. The bushfire season is no longer contained, stretching across the entire year in different parts of the country. The fires begin for any range of reasons – accident, arson, it doesn't matter. The heat is such that there is no containing them once they start. Just last week, I watched a fire raging out of control in Tasmania on the news. The screen of my television was lit up with flames and I listened to the journalist announce the death toll – over a hundred at that stage, closer to two hundred by the time the fire was finally overcome.

In my head, when I hear of people dying in Australia, I no longer react with uncomplicated sympathy. It's like there's a ticker in my mind now – I see every life lost as a space opening up for a refugee. How many people have to die before it's my family's turn to take their place?

I keep these thoughts quiet at work, conscious of my brown skin contrasted with the white of my colleagues. As time passes, I look more and more like the enemy. I button my lips and focus on blending in. But I can't stop putting out my photo frames each day. They are my motivation. The image of my grandparents, posed in front of the farmhouse they inherited from their British boss when he left Fiji, symbolises our resilience in the face of adversity. The photo of my cousins, grouped into a rough line in order of height, the two girls grinning with gap-toothed smiles, the two older boys slouching the way that teenagers do, shows me that I am not alone, that they are out there, waiting to join me. I need these photos.

I need them to remind me why I persevere.

On weekends, when I can take a break from immigration paperwork, I drive my electric car out to the national parks that fringe Canberra. Most of the parks have suffered greatly as a result of the changing climate – the dry heat was replaced with a humidity that changed the landscape, choking the fauna. Some areas have been so badly affected by drought and fires that they are closed to the public indefinitely. I rarely see kangaroos now. The lack of rain has meant not enough food and many have been culled to stop them from starving to death. When I do see roos, I stop in my tracks and stare at them, desperate to drink in their majesty.

I park my car at the visitor's centre at Namadgi National Park and pause at the foot of a walking track to read the warning signs: *By entering this park, you acknowledge the risk of sudden fire or flash flooding in areas of the park, and accept liability for any loss, injury or damage as a result of a natural disaster.*

I peer up the dirt track, fringed by low scrub on either side, trees rising out of the ground up ahead to create a shaded green tunnel. The warning could apply to anywhere now, mired as we are in climate disaster. I shrug my backpack onto my shoulders and stride out into the wilderness.

I always wanted to show my grandmother and my cousins the ways that Australia differs from Fiji. They could never comprehend the animals that we used to see routinely here – koalas and possums, echidnas, kangaroos. They are alien in Fiji.

Now I wonder if they will ever see marsupials frolicking in the grass. I want to take them out to a lookout and show them the dry and arid landscape of Canberra, the famous 'bush capital'. But that landscape barely exists anymore – it's a Legoland of buildings, apartments towering to the sky, office blocks lining every street. The urban sprawl has taken over the land and the concrete and tarmac are unable to absorb the heat the way that grass and dirt does, reflecting it back into the sky.

When I hear the shout, it takes a few moments to realise it is directed at me. The footpath is bare, a trickle of people strolling down the concrete carpet leading into the city centre. I turn and see a man on the other side of the road, his stance belligerent, his gaze aggressive.

'You heard me!' he calls. 'Go back to where you came from – we're full!'

A couple a few strides ahead of me falters, their backs stiff, but they don't stop or turn. My face feels hot, my heart rate fast. I turn away and keep walking, trying to ignore the prickling of my neck at the sensation of his gaze still locked onto me.

Thankfully, he doesn't yell again, and I keep walking, wooden now, like a puppet trying to perform the act of normalcy. I should be used to this. It happens more frequently than it used to but the attitude towards street harassment has irrevocably changed. Where once it was considered an aberration, something that shocked ordinary Australians, and would sometimes even elicit a stranger's response in my defence, now it's an ordinary part of our lives. I remember hearing a colleague talking about it once in our office kitchen. Her voice was hushed, and she glanced briefly my way, but it didn't stop her from saying what she thought. 'It's not really racist, though, is it?' she whispered to the white man in front of her. 'I mean, we really can't let more people in. We need to keep our resources for us.'

I wanted to be brave enough to say something then. I wanted to look her in the eye and say, 'I'm a citizen of Australia too. I've lived here, and paid my taxes, and contributed to our bounty, and I deserve to be here.' I wanted to say, 'You can't claim Australia without claiming the violence with which this land was taken. These resources belong to you as much as they belong to me, or anyone else who is a visitor here. By that, I mean they are not ours at all. They belong to First Nations communities. Who are you to decide how they are shared now?' But I didn't. My words died in my throat. I just huddled closer to the table, hunched over my lunch, trying to make myself as small as possible.

I do the same thing now, wrapping my arms around my waist as I walk faster, as if I'm fleeing the hovering remains of the man's words.

When I reach the city, I slow down and remember why I am here. It's the first Saturday of the month. The day that we meet, those of us who are left in Australia like the truncated limbs of our families still trapped in detention.

We meet in a quiet café, away from the main strip of eateries and restaurants that are usually crowded with white people. I used to frequent those places too. I had so many white friends, I would occasionally forget that I wasn't like them. But that was a long time ago. I can barely remember that version of me, of my life. Those people are long gone from my circles – or perhaps I'm gone from theirs. They might still see each other, but I no longer get the text messages, the invitations. It's just the way it is now. It doesn't make sense, when any moment could mean the end of my citizenship in favour of theirs.

The debate is still raging in parliament over whether the definition of 'Australian' needs to change, to close the ranks between migrants and white people, or to formalise the cultural ranking that has covertly existed for so long. I don't think it'll pass but the damage is already done. I'm no longer welcome in the places that I used to occupy: the arts festivals I used to love to attend, the high-end restaurants I would eat at with my friends, my cultural difference almost adding to their ambience. These places are no longer for me. I don't even mind anymore – I willingly sacrifice that belonging, if it means my family can finally leave the detention centre.

So this group started – a way for people like me to meet and share our anxiety and dread for our futures, for our families' safety, for the future of this country. We sit for a few hours and allow ourselves to share the feelings that we otherwise endure in isolation.

Today our gathering is sombre. Alena has had bad news. Her husband has been in the detention centre on Christmas Island for over a year, waiting to be allowed passage into the country. From Fiji as well, Alena came to Australia on a temporary work visa and has stayed illegally since it expired. Her husband, Silosi, applied for asylum, thinking he could join her here. They didn't consider the new arrangements that Australia has though, bargains struck with other First World countries to address their shared trouble with refugee intakes. Silosi has been granted asylum but he is going to be settled in Canada. He can choose to go back to Fiji but he is not coming to Australia.

Alena's face is ragged in the dim light of the café. 'I am as good as a widow now,' she says, shaking her head. 'We will die apart.'

'Can't you apply to go to Canada too?' one man pipes up, spreading his hands wide – the welcoming arms of a new country. But it's no use, if Alena is found out as an illegal immigrant, she will be put into indefinite detention and could face criminal charges. She is best to try and fade into the fabric of the country, to make herself small enough to pass unnoticed.

I sit quietly, like usual, not sure how to talk to these strangers, but still grateful for this small moment of solidarity. The gathering is coloured in the shades of multiculturalism – brown, olive, white, a tapestry of immigrants. Our alienation has ironically brought us together. If not for our shared precariousness, would we ever spend time with each other? I know that a decade ago, I would have tried hard to avoid being in a room like this, where I could be easily assumed to be more like *these people* than the *real Australians*. I was determined to have white friends, to differentiate myself from the immigrants who never assimilated. But my friends have dwindled these past years. I find myself no longer invited to weddings. The regular dinner invitations have gradually ceased, and I find it hard to connect with the friends I made in university, with everyone so busy now. I wonder if 'busy' is an excuse, the polite way of rejecting not just my friendship, but *me*. The rhetoric of difference has done its job and now I have to accept that no amount of wishing will make me less brown, less obviously *different*.

I sip my coffee and listen to Alena's grief, hoping that by sharing it I can lighten the burden somewhat. It is an empty hope but it is all we have left.

I dream deeply at night. It's as though the threads of my memory, flimsy in daylight, strengthen and tighten their hold on me in sleep. I can remember floating in the ocean, in my grandfather's boat. It was rickety, tin and wood, only big enough for me, him, and my father. I was small, young enough that I didn't understand the difference yet between my life in Australia and my family's existence in Fiji.

For child-me, my grandparents were alive only in the weeks that we visited Fiji – their lives turned off and on with my presence. The quaintness of their small house, the dirt roads, the lack of electricity at night, were all just strange holiday experiences for me. Their poverty was a backdrop to my brief moments in Fiji, and I didn't care or think about it when I was back in Australia, eating ice cream in front of the TV for the rest of my summer holidays.

But this day, it is clear in my mind as one of those pure memories, untouched and retained through decades of acquired knowledge. I can remember it sharply, and it is untainted. I remember the waves. I remember them lapping at the edges of the boat, the ocean accepting us and warning us gently with the controlled power of those pushes, those tugs. I remember the sun glinting off the water in thousands of individual points, my father shielding his eyes while squinting across the ocean. I remember the thin line of wire held in my grandfather's hand, a hook on the end, and a chunk of raw meat. I remember my father leaning forward with a cry of delight and scooping a starfish straight out of the water, holding it out for me to see.

'I want to keep it!' I said.

He shook his head. 'It belongs in the water.'

He let me cup my hand with his as we dipped our palms back into the sea and relinquished the creature to its depths.

The water was calm, unthreatening. I remember it. The sun, and the wind, and that rich smell of the sea. I hold onto the dream. If I could, I would never wake up.

Stitches Through Time

Sarah Ross

As you fly into Darwin city you can see the river systems that are carved in the earth in long thick lines that thin and curl at the end, like blood vessels that grow across lungs. The moment I crossed the threshold of the plane I felt the humid heat that hits you like a tidal wave, enveloping you and coating the inside of your chest, the humid heat that builds and builds and builds, like tension between lovers, before that tension is broken by distended storm clouds releasing the rain. The storms, coupled with the advancing and receding tides, are like the rhythmic rise and fall of lungs taking and releasing giant breaths of air. Every vacant space in Darwin is filled with coconut trees and palm trees. Vines creep over the yards to wind around clotheslines and fences while the residents of the apartments leave them undisturbed. They hang their clothes on the parts of the line that aren't yet overgrown. Geckoes make homes above the door frames, and the green tree frogs make their homes in the sinks and toilet. Ants line the windowsills and the freshly hatched golden tree snakes find their way through the bottom of doors and curl up in coffee cups and office administration trays. The frangipani trees form archways over the roads and their flowers fall to line the streets like white and yellow urban Broadway lights.

When I first moved to Darwin, I lived in a block of four units at the end of the intersection of Kurrajong and Palm streets. If you stood at the front door of my apartment at the mouth of Palm Street, you could see the glowing green leaves of the mangroves that grow on the Nightcliff foreshore. If you were to look at the building from the street, the units would resemble four shoe boxes stacked on top of each other, two by two. They had louvre windows on each outer wall that helped the breeze to ripple the stifling wet-season days and nights, and the inside and outside of the building was coated in cracked and textured creamy white paint. Each ground unit had a concrete porch at the front and back bordered by a dirt lot with shrubbery and palm trees, and on each back porch were an outdoor basin and washing machine. This was where I would mostly see the Filipino family from next door, as we loaded and unloaded our respective washing and hung it out to dry. My clothesline, in addition to the vine growth, had especially limited space as the upstairs neighbours kept a blue trailer underneath it which was often retrieved and returned by other members of the neighbourhood. The upstairs neighbours were two Punjabi families. At different times during the day I would hear devotional music, vibrant Bhangra beats, domestic disputes and loud phone calls in Punjabi that would overpower the Australian classic rock coming from adjacent apartment blocks and the Greek pop from across the road.

The sounds from the upstairs neighbours were usually coupled with pungent fragrances of turmeric, cumin and curry leaves that spilled over their balcony and floated through my bedroom window, invoking memories of home. Sometimes the woman upstairs would come downstairs and offer me paneer tikka in a kadai dish, urging me to 'take one more' and then again 'one more, one more'.

Lodging with the couple living directly above me was a taxi driver, Ranjik, who would park his taxi in my car space because he knew it irritated me. He would position the windscreen wipers of my car in the air as part of a series of amusing, albeit unreturned, gestures of romantic pursuit.

At the beginning of the wet, the Filipino family's furniture began to disappear and in its place appeared multicoloured butterfly-shaped fairy lights draped over the trees and small pot plants around the borders of the concrete porch. A chair and table appeared next to the front door along with an ashtray in the shape of a sunflower. The new tenant, Mary, had moved in after leaving her boyfriend. However, over the next few months he would often make visits, accompanied by the sound of screeching car tyres and broken glass. As the sun set, Mary was often on her porch blowing plumes of tobacco smoke among the shards of broken glass.

Many of the apartments in Nightcliff had large windows facing the street. At sunset, you could see people cooking, watching TV or sitting on their balconies in white singlets and hi-vis vests smoking cigarettes. In the wet season when the monsoons filled the city with rain, water ran in heavy streams down the gutters of the streets. On humid rainy days, amid the metallic smell of the asphalt and petrichor, I collected the fallen frangipani flowers and placed them in the gutter streams and watched them float down the road – white and yellow canoes floating down asphalt canals.

I was born on Whadjuk Noongar Boojar. The British called it the 'Swan River Colony' and then 'Perth' after the Scottish birthplace of the Secretary of State for War and the Colonies. My grandparents moved there when my mother was very young. She was born in the capital of West Bengal in northeast India. The British called it 'Calcutta' and after independence it was renamed Kolkata. My grandparents had the choice to go to England by ship or to Australia by plane. They were worried the children would fall through the rails of the ship, so they chose the plane. They arrived just after the White Australia policy was formally abolished – relatives who arrived only a few years before them had to prove they had a white relative in order to make the same journey. My grandparents, by virtue of time, did not have to do this. Their knowledge of English aided the approval of their visa.

My grandmother's mother, Josephine, was an orphan living in a Catholic convent as a ward of the bishop in Allahabad. No one knows how she ended up there; however, many of the mixed-race Indian children who had fair skin were brought to convents by extended white family members to be raised as European. She had jet-black hair, was short in stature and had a smile to suggest that she was concealing mischief. She was fluent in Urdu, Hindi and French.

My grandmother's father, Joseph, was born in Agra. He was a tall and towering man with dark brown skin and a voluminous moustache in the shape of an upside-down bow that he would curl upwards at the ends. He was employed by the British Indian Army. On a work visit to Allahabad he saw Josephine laying flowers on a memorial and made inquiries about her, subsequently bribing the bishop to seek permission to marry her. The bishop gave Josephine a choice – she could either get married or become a nun. A nun at the convent advised her to accept the proposal. 'Get married, child! Personally, I made a mistake becoming a nun.' This is the story I was told by Uncle Alfie. Uncle Alfie is their eldest son and, aside from my great-grandmother, had the greatest propensity towards mischief out of all the family. He was renowned for trading his school shoes for buffalo rides down the Yamuna River and acquiring pet monkeys and hiding them in the house. My grandmother tells me that Uncle

Alfie would commonly exclaim with profound indignation when accused of being untruthful, 'Thunder and lightning strike me dead if I am lying!' yet, she said, 'He was always frightened when there was a thunderstorm, he would close all the curtains and sit in the middle of the house.'

My grandfather's mother, Catherine, was a short and round woman from Kolkata. She had jet-black hair, brown-coloured skin and a proclivity to worry. She wore glasses with thick lenses that magnified the shape of her eyes. Her husband, Dennis, was a very rotund and broad-chested Scottish man with reddish-brown hair who worked at the wharf. They spoke to each other in Dennis's mother tongue. This is the language in which they spoke to their children and this is how the tether to language was lost. Great-grandmother Catherine would cook yellow dahl for her grandchildren when they visited on Saturdays and she'd sit across from them and attentively watch them eat. When they'd stop eating, her brows would crease together and her eyes widen, 'What's wrong? You don't like my cooking anymore?' When the carnival came to town, she'd anxiously twist her clothes with her hands, telling her grandchildren, 'Don't go on the rides! You know your money tin? I'll *double* the coins in there if you don't go on them! I'll cook your favourite food too!'

My white ancestors were our ticket to the colonial frontier, to stolen land, but my brown ancestors, like faceless ghosts, were the ones who linger behind me and whisper over my shoulder into my ear, 'You will never belong in this place, you can never leave us behind.'

When they settled in Perth, my grandparents worked long hours and attended night school. My grandmother would call my mum from work and talk her through the steps to prepare chicken curry, jalfrezi, fried okra and yellow dahl. From the age of ten, this was how my mum learnt to cook. She paid the bills, ran errands, cleaned the home and cared for her siblings. My mum and her siblings were put into Catholic schools so they could receive a Catholic education. If they talked during class their hands were caned with wooden rulers by reprimanding nuns. When she finished high school, my mum enrolled to study nursing. At that time, nursing students were required to live in the hospital where they were trained by nuns. Her first placement was in a children's ward and she was tasked with caring for a baby with failure to thrive – a baby who cried and cried and refused to sleep, eat or drink. Mum wanted to quit but the Mother Superior made her promise to see out the end of the month. Then my grandparents came to visit her, and they brought her fresh fruit, yellow dahl and Indian sweets: deep fried, glistening orange jalebis and brown syrupy gulab jamuns. She could not tell them she wanted to leave because she could not bring herself to disappoint them. That's how she ended up staying.

My grandfather always said whoever married my mum would be marrying gold. But my mum never married because she fell in love with her childhood best friend, Michelle. When I was conceived, same-sex couples were barred by law to have children through donors, however, through word-of-mouth my mothers found a doctor who at his discretion helped them conceive through an anonymous sperm donor. When they attended the initial appointment with him to choose a donor, my mum asked the doctor for a donor who was 'kind', 'generous' and had 'a good nature'. The doctor smiled and said that they couldn't choose those types of details, they could only choose hair colour, skin colour, height, build and education. My mother told me that Dr Russo was a very patient man who never placed time restrictions on their consultations. There is a photograph of me and him when I was a toddler. He has one arm around me and the other arm cradling my newborn brother. He is wearing a brightly coloured bow tie and a beige checked jacket. He has a large nose and brown eyes that crinkle with his wide toothy smile.

As a result of her Catholic upbringing, Mum felt shame at being gay and for being unmarried and pregnant. She feared that harm would come to her unborn child from divine retribution. When my mum's body was first wracked with the pains of labour, they didn't know how to explain my other mother's presence to the hospital staff.

My mothers read somewhere that the name Sarah means 'perfect'; I don't know where they read this because it actually means 'princess'. However, when I was delivered the first thing the doctor said upon seeing that I was healthy was, 'She's perfect,' and my mums turned to each other and said, 'Sarah.'

Mum's labour was exceptionally hard, difficult and dangerous yet she speaks about it with romantic reverence, 'As soon as I held you, it was all worth it. I would do it all again.' My other mother initially wasn't allowed into the theatre when Mum was being prepared for emergency postpartum surgery and she sat anxiously in the hallway. Then Dr Russo arrived and found her sitting in the hall. He took her into the theatre, gestured to my mum, and announced to all the staff, 'Wherever this woman goes, this woman goes too.' As my mum was recovering in hospital, the nurses educated her about contraception and social security came around to ask if she'd like to claim the payment for single parents.

When I was a child, we lived on a rural property. My mum would work in the garden while I played by the pool. I had a butterfly net that I used to scoop out drowning bees. I then placed them on the bark of a pineapple palm so they could dry out. I drew pictures of my family on the ceramic pool tiles. My younger brother had a different donor father and consequently inherited his father's fair complexion and crystal-blue eyes. I coloured the skin of my mum and me in black permanent marker and left the fairer skinned family members as unfilled white outlines.

The first time I was asked, 'Where are you from?' was in kindergarten. I was one of a handful of brown children in the entire school. We were tasked with drawing side profiles of our faces and I reduced the size of my Indian nose so it sat less obtrusively, less curved, and less prominent, like the rest of the children in the class.

Then I saw myself reflected in an image other than my own: I was given a book by my mother called *Death of a Princess*; a fictional story set in Ancient Egypt. I held the book in my hands and looked with amazement at the girl on the cover – the almond shape of her eyes, the curve of her long nose, the fullness of her lips and the coffee colour of her skin. I didn't understand that I was not Egyptian, all I understood was that the girl in the photograph looked like me, and it was the first time I had seen my physical features reflected in any type of book or story. It made me feel special, like I shared something with this character that my classmates did not. Maybe there was another place or another world where people looked like me.

One day in art class we were instructed to make Father's Day cards. I felt nervous and walked up to the teacher and gestured for her to bend down closer towards me so I could whisper close to her ear, 'I don't have a dad … I have two mums.' I always had butterflies in my stomach at parent–teacher days, wondering if one or both of my mothers would come. I worried that they would hold hands at the school and the other kids would see. I recollected with discomfort Jesse Jamieson sitting next to me on the limestone border of the playground and asking me if my mum was a 'homosexual'. I had seen him whisper into the ears of other children while looking at me. I didn't know what that word even meant but I knew that I had only ever heard it in tones conveying insults or disgust. I didn't want to hurt my mothers' feelings, so I kept my discomfort a secret.

When I was growing up, I rejected the church because it became apparent that it was hostile to the existence of my family. One morning when Mum was driving us to school our car was flooded with a crackled reading of Pope John Paul II's 'Considerations': 'Allowing children to be adopted by persons living in same sex unions would actually mean doing violence to these children, in the sense that their condition of dependency would be used to place them in an environment that is not conducive to their full human development.' We listened to it in the same way you hear white noise in the background, it wasn't turned down or censored, it was just a backdrop to the world we lived in. Then in the evening as my brother and I played on the floor with our toy plastic dinosaurs, our bulky black television flooded the lounge room with the voice of the Prime Minister, John Howard: 'Marriage … is a union between a man and a woman … If you allow unions between men and men or women and women to be given the same status, it will over time erode the value and therefore erode the special character … of marriage.' As an adult I learnt that many of the anti-gay laws were biproducts of British anti-sodomy laws inherited from colonisation. My mother never reconciled with the church but continued to maintain her own independent relationship with God.

I heard a plover screeching overhead as I sat on the grass of the foreshore on a steaming hot wet-season afternoon. I sat watching the deep blues of the ocean and the white and grey storm clouds that stretched from the horizon to the sky like mountainous and cascading cotton skyscrapers. The wet seasons had become hotter and hotter year by year. The storms and cyclones were coming with increased frequency. I held knitted mauve wool in my hands and ran my fingers over its fibrous texture. My grandmother had taught me how to knit when I was eleven. Now it had been a year since she passed away. She would sit in her chair and I would kneel down on the floor beside her, resting one forearm on her knee. I remember looking at her very long, bony, brown and wrinkly, but soft like velvet fingers, as she showed me how to tie the first stitch on the needle. She then took the mauve-coloured wool and showed me how to use the first stitch to create the subsequent stitches. If I dropped a stitch and continued to knit, it would create a hole in the piece. I would give it back to her and she would yell at me in a high-pitched shriek, 'What is this? What have you done?' She would take the stitches off the needle and pull at the wool to undo all the lines that had already been knitted together, all my painstaking work, until she reached the place where the mistake was made and repaired it. She had always wished to visit the Taj Mahal one last time before she died.

India is a land of God. It is in every person, stitched in the seams of the street, tucked in the corners of buildings and placed in the windows of every shop and every home. In the river that runs through the ancient city of Agra, there are framed pictures of God on the rocks and river bank. People place offerings of flowers at the foot of the images, and these flowers wash into the water and float past when you are wading in the water. The river holds space for prayer, bathing and washing clothes. Some clothes have slipped away and become stuck in the rocks of the riverbed, metres and metres of sarees flowing with the water. I felt them beneath my feet when I crossed the river. To get to Agra, I boarded a train from the Delhi railway station. I wandered the carriage, uncertain of where to sit and too shy to ask anybody to move. The carriage was overcrowded and bodies filled every spare space on the seats and pieces of luggage dotted the aisle.

A young girl on a single seat watched me. She wore her long black hair in a plait down her back and sported a blue churidar, a loose tunic top with leggings. She leaned over to the back part of the carriage and said 'aunty' followed by something in Hindi and a woman who had been lying down across the seat sat upright to make room for me. In India, everyone you address is generally referred to as 'aunty', 'uncle', 'sister', 'brother', 'mother' or 'father'. The reclining woman to the left of me was part of a group of three aunty-aged women all dressed in sarees. They spoke loudly and with great animation but I had no idea what they were saying. Their feet reached across the space between the seats and rested in the spaces between each other, however, should they touch another's foot with their own, they apologetically touched their hand to their heart and forehead. This was because people are considered to be divine to Hindus and it is disrespectful to touch a divine being or object with one's feet.

The carriage was very hot. There were small pedestal fans bolted to the ceiling which added to the breeze from the open windows, unlike the air conditioning units in the first and second class carriages. It was 45 degrees Celsius and you could see a film of sweat on the brown faces of everyone in the carriage. Every woman was wearing a saree or a salwar kameez and the very few men in the carriage were all dressed in white cotton kurtas.

Several more people boarded the train including an older woman and a young boy. The older woman was wearing a yellow and orange saree. Her grey hair with remnants of black was pulled back into a bun but the heat and breeze from the open windows caused some strands to stand on end. One of her eyes had a pale blue cataract and stared vacantly while her other one moved around the carriage. Her skin was golden brown and weathered with tattoos that had bled from the lines with age. The boy, who I assume was her grandson, was gripping onto her hand. He was wearing beige, slightly too large shorts and a blue button-up shirt. He was carrying a 600ml Coca-Cola bottle with a small amount of clear water inside.

Although I was unsure what she was saying, it was clear that the grandmother was instructing people where to sit and to make room for each other. She pointed to particular seats and pieces of baggage and people moved their bodies and objects accordingly. The train began moving again. The grandmother nodded her head at my water bottle. I handed it to her. She poured the last of my water into her grandson's Coca-Cola bottle and encouraged him to drink. Another few aunties came into the carriage and squeezed into the bench I was seated on. Their bodies pressed up against my side, mingling the sweat from our skin. I was hot and uncomfortable, I wanted to tug at my clothing but my arms were pinned, however I found the forced closeness and familiarity endearing and oddly comforting. I was crushed-up against the window to the point that I couldn't move. Farming fields moved like a reel of film outside the window: yellow, parched and dry, while the barefoot, shirtless farmers wearing dhotis and makeshift turbans moved like skeletal ghosts churning dust with their sickles-and-bone-thin cattle. The grandmother said something to the aunty directly next to me, who was pressing me against the window, and pointed her open palm towards me, and the aunty moved to allow me more space. Elders in India are treated with reverence, as are guests. I heard the grandmother say, 'Agra'.

'Agra?' I repeated. She nodded. I put my hand to my chest to indicate that Agra was also my stop. She spoke towards me when we approached Agra and we both rose. She looked at the luggage rack to make sure I didn't forget any of my bags. The sky glowed purple, blue and indigo as the sunrise floated over the rim of the horizon, illuminating the creamy marble crown and crescent moon of the Taj Mahal and the muddy banks of the Yamuna River. The river was brown, and slightly polluted. The land around it was dry and dusty. Bare-chested, brown-skinned men wrapped in dhotis raked irrigation ditches in the earth to sow fresh golden wheat crops under cotton shade cloths. Women clad in red and yellow sparkling sarees with baskets poised on their heads and braids billowing down the crevices of their backs, carrying and shifting rubble to rebuild the ruins on the banks and to clear it of the ebbing plastic waste.

I sat on the boundary wall of the Taj Mahal and slipped my hand in my bag. I cradled the wool knitted by the hands of my grandmother as I watched amid the backdrop of the rubble and dust, standing timeless and unblemished.

Ostraka.

Claire G. Coleman

The sun is in its place and in this place the sun is like no other I have ever seen. Yesterday when they brought a man here, when he first felt the sun's heat, he had swooned, they had to carry and drag him into the cage. He has not woken yet, I am told, their petty revenge for the extra effort they had to make delivering him has left him half dead. A thing of meat, cooking in the tin-shed infirmary, he is unlikely to ever wake; I don't expect him to join me out here where I am.

I am stateless now, the law, the cops, border patrol has taken me from me, from place, from my country; left me with no country, no home, at all. I am within bars, not bars, the bars are metaphorical, I lean face first against a chain-link fence. I do not know what is outside, but bush, thicker than I have seen, thicker than I am capable of imagining.

That is how I know this is not a nightmare, or if it is; it's not mine. I would, therefore, desire to give this vision back to whoever owns it.

I am leaning face first against a fence, still the bush is too far away to properly smell it. It's too hot to stand there in the clear space before and beyond the fence – they cleared the life from before me so they can watch the wire – but I cannot drag myself away.

I can smell my sweat cooking.

Along the fence a man mumbles on a loop, I can hear the pattern, I can hear his voice rising and falling, but I cannot make out any words. He was there yesterday too. I can't remember if he was there the day before but it seems likely. He's even thinner than me, all cooked and starved down to skin and bone, I know the moment he stops mumbling he will mummify. I told the guards about him yesterday and they didn't care, or was it the day before. Should I mention it again today, or should I wait until tomorrow, those are the difficult questions; those are the only questions I am allowed to ponder here.

Tomorrow he might be dead, desiccated and silent, but to help him would risk my wellbeing; and yet to do nothing would risk my soul; risk the last vestige I have of me, the conviction that I am a good person ...

Yet, the guards don't like being made to do anything, or think, or care, or act human.

I push myself away from the fence and it twangs, there are dents in my skin where my weight pushed my loosening skin, my scrawny flesh and bones too hard against the wire. If I am not careful the wire-dents in my skin will become permanent, a lasting impression of my place here. Then, this place and I will be one and I will never leave.

I will never leave.

I try and saunter to the building containing the common room and the office. I have not sauntered for a while and have lost the knack but it's such a great word that I consider the matching action worth attempting. Any way of moving, other than slinking, is difficult when all movement must be from shade of tree to shade of building to shade of tree. There are places where open sky must be crossed, where the sun might kill anyone not careful enough.

In those places people swelter, which has a similar sound but is not close to the same thing. Someone is face down in the sun. I try to help them stand but they refuse. I get too hot trying; almost swoon myself. I stagger the rest of the way.

The office is locked but outside, in the thin shade of the verandah, I see the crate with the mail in it is full. I have complained about it before, the mail being left there where anyone can steal it, where careless digging can perform unintended liberations of people's mail on to the floor where letters can be kicked into hidden places or trampled unreadable underfoot; or stolen by the wind. Fortunately few, if any, prisoners have discovered the mail is in.

I am more careful than some others will be, I dig through calmly, almost enjoying it, searching for letters with my name on them. There's nothing near the top, I remove the top layer and check it meticulously – taking care to forget the names as soon as I read them – pile the letters even more carefully. I collect the next layer down and read the name on every letter. Nothing for me there either.

I have made two neat piles with nothing for me in them.

Finally near the bottom of the box, a simple business-size envelope with my name on it and that is all, I secret the letter in my clothes, even now after they have let me take it from the crate they could confiscate it. Or someone could steal it, just to hurt me or to make me buy it back with precious smuggled luxuries.

Back in my room, in my shed the size of a cell, the size of a double bed and no bigger, I sit on my hard-as-wood, narrow-as-me bed. I am lucky, in a way, circumstance and danger has earned me a room on my own, I can lock the door, keep everyone but the guards at bay.

I savour the letter before I open it, brushing my fingers across the smooth paper of the envelope, read my name again and again, closing my eyes and opening them so they can again be surprised by its presence; even raising the unopened letter to my nose to smell it. It takes more strength than I thought I had to resist licking it.

Finally, there is nothing to do but open it, slowly, I make a game of trying not to tear any of the envelope; peeling back the flap millimetre by slow millimetre. I listen with full concentration to the sound of the contents slipping out of the envelope; unfold the paper slowly with my eyes closed so I don't catch an accidental early view of what the letter says.

I let my eyes open; I don't know if I can keep them closed any longer.

There's my name, after 'dear', there's the three neat paragraphs I would expect from a business or legal letter. No surprises there but I can still hope to find a pleasant shock in the contents.

I read quickly, unable to prolong the effort to my satisfaction.

My lawyer is coming to see me.

Tomorrow.

I cannot decide whether to jump out of my skin with excitement or cry with terror.

I decide instead to go to bed, to sleep. Whether tomorrow is exciting or terrifying; the best thing I could do is to make it come faster by sleeping. The second-best thing I could do is to get some sleep and be well-rested. I close my eyes so I don't stare at the ceiling; grey unpainted metal, no ceiling at all, just the roof of the shed my room clearly is.

No matter how I try I cannot sleep, I fall down a hole towards memory but I cannot hold the memories either; assaulted by flashes of my time before the island, before the prison. There were people I can now barely remember, a job I am not sure I liked, people I loved, a house, a car. I hated my pile of junk car back then but now I miss it like a recently lost lover, I mourn it like a dead child. I can't even remember what model it was but I remember it was white between the rust.

It's a long night of alternation between staring at the ceiling and staring at the inside of my eyelids; a long night of sweaty heat and the squalling of night birds. Then I wake when the sun is blasting through the window of my room; tickling my face, tugging at my eyes.

I have no watch, no phone, no way but the sun and the movement of guards to check the time; I do not even recall having seen a timepiece in this place, this concentration camp, this prison, this hell-hole; my home. No, I refuse to see it as my home. Yes, it's now my home, I have nowhere else.

Rolling out of bed I wish I had more clothes than the stinking, sweaty, loose pants and t-shirt I am wearing; which are the only clothes I own. I have lived in them, slept in them, done everything in them for … well I don't even know how long I have been here in this place. I do know that my clothes have been replaced after falling to pieces many times with outfits that are essentially identical but for their newness.

I don't know what time it is but the sun is high enough in the sky, the heat forceful enough, that I know I have overslept. None of the guards woke me this morning; normally they would blast us awake with noise, intentional, or pretending it's an accident. I hope I am not too late for visiting hours.

Rushing across the blowtorch-hot compound I dodge from shade to shade, already dripping with sweat, flies and other hateful flying things dive-bombing my eyes to steal my tears. I ignore the mosquito bites, the small flies miscalculating and getting stuck to my sweat, the laughing guards, the cold sweat on my back, the heat on my face.

There are people, if I can call such shabby, scabby skeletons people, milling around against a fence. On the other side of that fence is a space between fences, scattered with institutional plastic chairs and soggy paper. In there, below the looming razor-wire, under the dispassionate eyes of cameras, the visitors should be gathering so we, the prisoners, can talk to them through the fence.

But there is nobody there, on the other side of the wire, only empty fallen chairs that await them. I am too early.

I stretch my arms as far apart as they can go along the fence, grip tight like someone crucified; press my face so hard against the wire I can feel it bruising. There I will wait, while my fingers lock themselves painfully to the steel, while my face tries to become one with the fence, while my back blisters in the sun; even through clothes.

My name sneaks insistently into my ears and lights a match in my brain. I start to fight out of a hole I did not know I had fallen into; my thoughts feel like someone has staked them down.

My lawyer is white, his skin, the visible hair implants on his balding head, are glowing unpleasantly in the sunlight in a way that tells me he's going to regret being out there before long. I imagine those implants will itch tomorrow, the skin between them is already bright red and furious.

'I have looked further into your case,' my lawyer says with a voice like a briefcase lock. 'It's unprecedented, this situation, and there are some questions as to whether it's constitutional and whether it is supported by international laws and treaties but frankly, there seems to be little we can do.'

My voice comes to me like the hiss of escaping steam, 'I can't be left stateless, there must be something that can be done.' I know I sound scared; I look over to make sure nobody else can hear it.

To my left is a woman as scrappily dressed as I am, talking through the wire at a lawyer so like mine I don't know how I tell them apart. Her lawyer has a folder of papers, I look down and see mine does too, why did I not notice? And she, the detainee, looks like she should be as white as her lawyer but in the sun of that place she's the colour of a boiled lobster.

Something is tickling my ears and I realise it's words. I turn back to my lawyer and his mouth is moving, '... the law has long enabled them to indefinitely lock illegal immigrants, even refugees in detention, anybody ...' Then I am moving on, to the person to my right.

He has a beard that twenty-five years ago would have been fashionable but in this place is simply a clue he has been here a long time. He's shirtless, stupid, he wears proud blisters on his back like he plans to burn himself to death in protest without a fire. His beard and hair are ginger, he's almost on fire already, I wonder if he feels the heat of his hair; I wonder if it will cook his brain; wonder if it already has. His lawyer is a woman, and has a tablet not papers, but besides that is indistinguishable from mine.

The sun is too hot, I cannot concentrate on my lawyer's words, they are too big anyway and they keep joining the utterances of the other lawyers, forming alliances and picking fights. And I remember.

I was comfortable in an armchair in an airline members lounge, I was not alone but I cannot remember who I was with. A glass of wine was in my hand, all the wine I could ever want was free, to make the flights more comfortable. There was so much food, there was cheese; god I miss cheese. That world seems alien now.

I boarded a delayed plane to a conference; complained about the delay like being stuck at an airport was an unmitigated disaster and not just a First World problem. Then, meetings, talking, too many people who didn't matter and nowhere near enough time with the few people who did matter. I can't remember anymore which country I was in, all countries are the same when all I see are conference venues, airports, the entrails of planes, taxis, hotel rooms.

It's a small world when you travel within those spaces, every hotel is the same hotel, every plane is the same plane and so on; monotonous and deliriously dull.

I returned in a plane, once inside it, it could have been any plane; once I landed it could have been any airport. Passport in hand I stopped at immigration; staffed heavier than I had ever seen it; walls of suits, of uniforms, of whiteness and control. I handed over my passport, I was taken to a small room silent but for the sound of air sneaking down the ducts.

A suit that may or not have had something inside it came in, a hand that was so indistinct as to be indistinguishable from all other hands took my passport and examined it at length. That suit left without talking to me, another came in, later on I was no longer sure it was a different suit at all.

They left; left me there. I don't remember how long I sat there, in that room, windowless, intentionally plain; so quiet the air in the ducts were as loud as a shout. I couldn't resist, I tried the door, it was locked, no amount of force could get it opened. I resisted the urge to release the scream I could feel rising.

Hours later they came, bound my hands tourniquet-tight with cable ties. I already didn't know what to do with my hands; I don't know what they thought I was planning. 'Where are you taking me?' I yelled; 'Where are we going?' I yelled; 'Do you know who I am?' I yelled. Maybe they knew who I was because they referred to me by name, they used my name, as they dragged me bodily, bloodily, bound, onto a Hercules.

People I recognised from the conference and from the plane were there; we were all too piss-pants terrified to talk to each other, to discuss what was happening.

There had been no way to talk on the plane once it departed, the engine noise made it almost impossible; nobody was talking to us anyway, none of us wanted to talk to each other. It was a voiceless, noisy trip to who knew where.

They had brought me to this place, this fenced compound, these sheds they called cabins, this jungle; inhospitable hell. I can't even remember how long ago that was.

The drone of my lawyer brings me back to the prison, the fence, the present.

'I was born in Australia, I have citizenship, I have no other citizenships, they can't leave me stateless.' I am squeaking like a door.

'They did,' says my lawyer with a sigh, his breath is shallow, like he is already dead, and my eyes are burning with tears I will not acknowledge.

'You were declared a 'person of bad character', the country's new law, the 'Ostraka' law of 2039, allows people of bad character to be ostracised, they have declared the precedent set in the Athenian Democracy valid. Someone ostracised is no longer a citizen, it's effectively exile. We have challenged the law, many of us have.' My lawyer has a voice like water boiling in a saucepan. 'They have not managed to remove anybody yet, under the new laws, but they got you as you returned to the country. Once ostracised you arrived here as a non-citizen, an illegal immigrant. I have it here,' he says, holding out a photocopy, 'your ostraka.'

'What do I do?' I squeal like a whistling kettle.

I can barely understand him through the screaming in my ears, he rolls up a form from his folder small enough to pass it through the wire, I snatch it before the guards can appear. Once it is in my hand I know they could not, would not take it; I know that rule well. I unroll the paper; read the title, 'Character Reference Form 1' it says.

'Fill this in with the right names, I will be back tomorrow to collect it,' he says in a bored tone. 'I have to leave the island tomorrow or I risk an ostraka myself.'

I stare at him, a metallic taste in my mouth like I have been sucking on the fence.

'All my friends,' I choke out of my lungs, 'all my friends, anybody who might give me a character reference, are in here.'

He shrugs, says, 'I have others to see,' then turns away.

I turn too, back towards the middle of the compound; towards my shed, my cabin, where I now know I will be spending the rest of my life; a form I have no use for gripped in my hand like it matters.

Buto

(Tagalog, noun:

bone, seed)

Kaya Ortiz

ossify

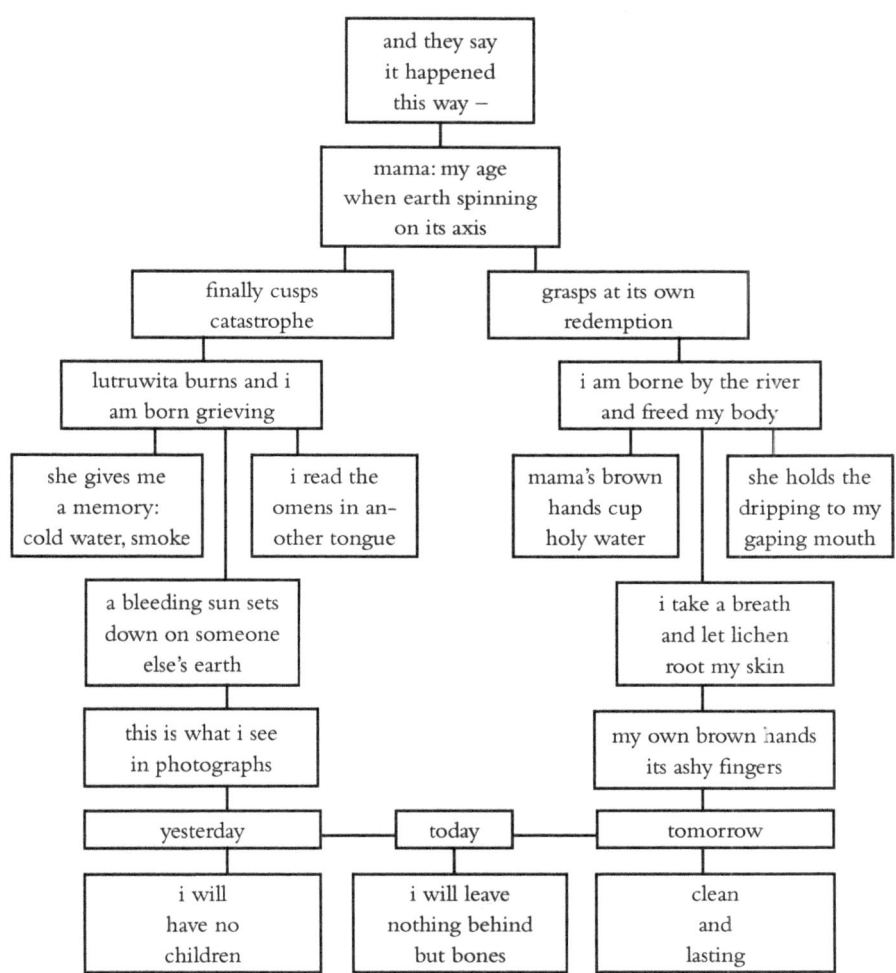

and they say
it happened
this way –

mama: my age
when earth spinning
on its axis

finally cusps
catastrophe

grasps at its own
redemption

lutruwita burns and i
am born grieving

i am borne by the river
and freed my body

she gives me
a memory:
cold water, smoke

i read the
omens in an-
other tongue

mama's brown
hands cup
holy water

she holds the
dripping to my
gaping mouth

a bleeding sun sets
down on someone
else's earth

i take a breath
and let lichen
root my skin

this is what i see
in photographs

my own brown hands
its ashy fingers

yesterday

today

tomorrow

i will
have no
children

i will leave
nothing behind
but bones

clean
and
lasting

swallow

july. the blossoms are early.
i speak to tatay on the holo-phone.
his accent like home, mine
thick as sikwate.

    tell me about the rain this year.
not much, but it snows sometimes.
    how's malaya?
floating / verdant / lost / ephemeral.

        once, before i am mother,
        tatay guts a fish in the sink.
        i grate a brown coconut,
        squeeze the soft flesh into
        milk. years drip white
        between my fingers.

    how many?
thirty / twenty / ten / none.

malaya – free
(as in i name her what i am)
one letter removed from

malayo – far
(as in chasms too wide
for reaching)
(as in i never go back)
(as in displacement is
blood-bitter on my tongue,
and still i swallow)

at the store, i tick boxes
on a screen: okra, kangkong,
bitter melon, rice, bok choy.
tins of synthetic spam, corned beef.
the bag comes out on a conveyer belt.
i press my finger to the pad and pay.

      but once: i pick malunggay
      off the tree, pull the bones
      from fried fish. green mango
      encrusted in salt. at noche
      buena – roast pig centrepiece,
      brown skin crisp-cracking. oil
      pooling on the plate. my mouth
      a flood – i crunch, i swallow.

how long now?
until what?
until spring. until the swallows come.

i hold my tongue, swallow
and taste salt. i picture
islands plunged into pacific,
and everything lost
is mine.

what next?
extinction. or the days
conveyer-belted this way,
until, until, until.

august. the blossoms pink
on the trees, birdsong.
i look and imagine the sun,
not-burning / burning on.
no matter the soft seep
of time like tea leaves
in water.

outside, a swallow
makes home, back from

a warmer climate.
i sip my tea, i swallow.
no matter, no matter.

the swallow always
comes.

kunanyi

i am as old
    as the river
timtumili minanya
    carving viridian country
echo of whale-song
    from its frigid depths

i fallow / i rust /
    i burn / i breathe out
organ pipe dolerite
    cleave winter snowfall
sprout twisted
    snow gum from soil

i, too, am a body
    browned by sun
rooted and
    watching
nipaluna sprawled
    and urban below

the city remembers
    nothing but

what the fire stokes
    or takes away
what legacy is theirs
    to name

i know the silence
    before the dark
lost world cascades
    into twilight
the river quiet now
    the sky clear

there is only the sun's
    rise and fall
what i remember
    from long ago
what i will be left
    to forget

i watch the future / past
    / present unfold
ask me again
    what i see
and i will say, everything
    everything

whole/hole/holy

1. once, everything was whole.

2. they are digging a hole through the earth. hills burnt and turned to dust.

3. i first kissed alina on the mountain. from the paths and crags of lost world, we emerged witness to the city, the river, the lurching landscape.

4. all land is sacred, but nowhere holier than this.

3. i kissed her. we had nothing more to lose.

5. i speak to my mother in spatters of bad tagalog. i tell her i am gay. i don't say that i'm afraid.

6. i take alina east to larapuna – to the clear blue water, the rust-lichened slabs of rock uneroded by tides.

7. there is always something bigger, something older than we are.

8. we lie in the sun despite the hole in the atmosphere, two brown bodies pretending our melanin will save us.

4. all land is sacred, but nowhere holier than this.

8. the word 'hole' is too small for what racks the atmosphere: an ever-widening chasm of depleting ozone.

5. mama gives me an umbrella, tells me to stay out of the sun.

2. the word 'hole' is too small for what they are digging: underground shelters to protect us from ultraviolet radiation. eventually, to save us from the heat.

7. we pollinate fear or hope. i cannot tell the difference.

2. my body is holy, but they will bury me before i'm gone.

9. at home, my parents watch on a holo-screen as typhoons raze their islands.

10. i imagine my ancestors; their bones beneath earth i've never touched.

10. i imagine my ancestors. the body that holds me to them – mine, yet unknown to me.

7. i am south of everything i do not know. i watch as it wanes away.

4. all land is sacred, but nowhere holier than this.

1. once, we too were whole.

THERE IS NO RIGHT ANSWER

true or false

T / F | brown skin on brown skin is revolution

T / F | girl laced with girl is cosmic revelation

T / F | brown girl is revel / evolution / elevation

fill in the blanks

1. i am a hundred thousand islands _____
   (uninhabited fractured drowning forgotten)
2. she is the gap between _____ and atmosphere
   (skin smoke light water)
3. we are a consequence of _____
   (collision immigration rainfall reckoning)

question / answer

1. where does a body end / where does it begin

2. what is truth / what is the acid on your tongue

3. is this dying thirst / is this hollow hunger

multiple choice

we begin:

    a.   beneath the shade of a gum tree

    b.   permeate as coal

    c.   seed burnt and splintered open

    d.   knowing nothing

    e.   heterogenous

we end:

    a.   in the dark

    b.   [   ]

    c.   one last supernova

    d.   bodies warm and falling

    e.   irradiated

in every iteration, the same story:

    a.   open palms cracking like dry earth

    b.   plastic floating across the sea

    c.   truth is time is construct is

    d.   nothing between us but empty atoms

    e.   we are we are we are we are

genesis

this world, we know.
this world, we make and
she gives us back our names.

      we are unburied and clean.

listen.   every lost thing will
                  be found: arctic glaciers
                  age-old trees of takayna

                  the great barrier reef
                  the story of the mountain
                  what song the river sings

                  your grandfather's handwriting
                  a holy leather-bound book
                  an heirloom gold ring

listen.   today, we understand.
                  language lives: in the trees –
                  in the balete and the snow gum

in the dolerite and sandstone
in the mouth of a milkfish
in a swallow's soft trill

nothing here is strange.
a border unravels, bears witness.
i see your skin. i call this kinship.

i give you a bleeding mango
heart. you give me a memory
wrapped in banana leaves.

we are myth translated into truth:
a body is history made visceral
a reversal – the ancient made new.

this future, this now, this
imperfect continuous present
this new, this on and on and on and –

this is how we ossify: we wax
diurnal. we eat with our hands. we
remember: we belong to the land.

Black Thoughts

Horses
and Mules

Hannah Donnelly

There is a lonely backwards town I often drive through called Uralla in the New England Tableland of northern New South Wales. I get to the flat town of Uralla driving over the mountains of the Great Dividing Range on a road called Thunderbolts Way. The place is famous because Captain Thunderbolt, one of New South Wales's last bushrangers, used a cluster of old granite boulders there to hide while he surveilled passing coaches to rob. Captain Thunderbolt, the gentleman bushranger, was cornered and shot by a constable near Uralla in 1870. His grave in the old general cemetery is a site of state significance. In the true Australian tradition of honouring anyone that killed, stole or claimed something that wasn't theirs, Captain Thunderbolt has a statue near the tourist information centre. The glorious bronze bearded larrikin on the back of a rearing stallion winks at those brave enough to look.

I have been stuck in Uralla twice. The first time was with my mum and sister when the ailing Ford Falcon broke down. We stayed in a noisy room above the pub, crowded in one bed that hadn't had its hideous fringed coverlet changed since Thunderbolt was shot. The other time was an end to my own crime spree. I was desperate and agreed to carry illicit substances for a group of fellows, definitely not a criminal bikie gang, that I was associated with, for a good bit of money. Instructions were to travel to Glebe to pick up some 'coffee' from a supplier, they would provide me with a car, and I would drive it to the drop location at a clubhouse eight hours across the state. Simple, really. Drive an unregistered car with a suspended licence and a couple Ks of amphetamines in the boot down Thunderbolts Way and horaah, off we go in joyful strains of 'Advance Australia Fair'. The authorities caught up with me at the Uralla service station across the road from Thunderbolt's gaze while I was getting some fuel.

This is how I remember it. A highway patrol car slowed down to a roll, window down on the passenger side. A bulky mass leaned out. 'Miss Donnelly,' he says politely, 'I have to speak with you.' He chucks a U-y and I just stand there stupidly wondering how this cop knows my name. All of a sudden he's pulled up next to me, leaping out of his car, already on his radio calling my details into the station. This bung-eyed fat cop tells me he is Constable Fuckhead and he is gonna search my car. Well, he doesn't find any amphetamines because as if I would ever be a drug mule, what kind of idiot would think that? I fake cry and tell him he's got it all wrong. I didn't receive the letters in the mail notifying me of my unpaid fines for parking longer than five minutes in Bondi. I didn't know that my car was unregistered or that my licence was suspended. I was just on my way back to visit my parents who needed my help. I can really spin some goona on the fly: truth is, it's just not in my DNA to pay fines. My dad always said white people haven't paid the rent, so why should I?

The good constable didn't believe me. Said only a drug mule would be driving an unregistered car across the country. I'd been flagged. He wouldn't let me get back in the car, and I was lucky he didn't drag me off to lock up. He watched suspiciously from his highway patrol car as I walked down the road to the dodgy pub I'd been in with Mum years ago, the proud owner of a new galaxy-sized fine. Constable Fuckhead stayed the whole night to make sure I didn't escape in my unregistered car. I don't think he ever worked so hard in his life. The next day Dad had to come from Inverell to pick me up. On the drive home Dad was geeing me up to go to court to dispute the fines. He has never paid for any of his multiple traffic infringements or penalties, he has fronted to the local magistrate every time.

It's taken a decade, but I've finally paid off all my fines, the penalties accrued over time, plus all the other gifts Constable Fuckhead gave me. I took the coward's way out instead of stepping into a court to ask for justice from crooks. These days I try to avoid statues of Australian heroes and bushrangers, so I don't get mixed up with worshipping trickster spirits and cursed men.

List of
Known
Remedies

Khalid Warsame

In less than a week my first poetry collection would be released. It was out of my hands now and all I had to do was stay alive until the next one. I was considering how to spend my morning when Sam called me and asked if I could drive him and Meteor to the vet.

'What happened to Meteor?'

'He swallowed a beer bottle cap,' said Sam. Every time I thought of Meteor, I couldn't help but imagine my Ayeeyo's reaction to the idea of a therapeutic dog. When I was eight or nine, I told her that I wanted a dog for my birthday and she turned to my mother and said, 'Look at what your child is saying.' She said it in English, so that my mum could understand, and it was one of the only memories I had of her.

'He'll appreciate you coming to see him,' said Sam. He had adopted Meteor the previous spring on the advice of his therapist, who told him that the unconditional love of a pet would do him good. I found the logic dubious. Sam was stuck in a gruelling clinical psychology PhD and was working part-time as a substitute high school teacher, and the last thing he needed in his life was a dog, particularly one like Meteor. He was an absolute disaster of a dog, a nervous wreck, and prone to bite or throw up at any moment. The throwing-up was particularly messy. Meteor's sensitive bowels were a rich vein of misery for Sam, who, after an exhaustive process of trial and error, determined that Meteor would only eat a specific Swedish brand of dog food called KILMAT. Sam shipped it in bulk from Sweden via New Zealand to get around the trade embargo – and bought a second fridge to store it all – but Meteor wasn't even halfway through his supply when he decided that he didn't eat KILMAT anymore. On top of this, Meteor was also a natural escape artist. Once, after a lively encounter with another puppy at the dog park, Meteor stopped and, guided by an esoteric signal, sensed the momentarily ajar gate behind him. He spun around and shot off, squeezing between a woman's legs. Meteor ignored the startled rottweiler beside the woman, which was as surprising as the escape itself since Meteor never passed up an opportunity to sniff a new dog's butt, and he disappeared down the street. Sam and I combed West Footscray together that evening and were about to head to my place to design and print some lost dog flyers when Sam gave a shout. A moment later Meteor crashed into me. I tried my best to throw him off, and he nearly got me this time. Before I could put some distance between us, Meteor bounded off again, this time with my hat in his mouth. Sam ran off after him, eventually catching up to

Meteor at a bus stop, but the damage was done; I would never see that hat in one piece again.

The first review for my poetry collection had come out the day before in *Thermometer*, written by a critic I hadn't heard of named Paul Strongman. The name struck me as a highly aggressive one for a critic, but I was lucky to have even one review, so I savoured reading it. The review was measured but positive, characterising the poem 'Dionne Brand' as an 'attempt to wrestle with the anxiety of influence', which sounded wild to me. I called that poem 'Dionne Brand' because I was reading her book *Inventory* while listening to Young Thug and I thought it would be a cool idea to change the titles of some of my poems to the names of poets. I sent a link of the review to Rosie and she responded immediately, quoting the least charitable line, '… scattered, but with much promise …', followed by several knife emojis. Her response – the speed, the informality of it – thrilled me. This was a new thing, a new and strange thing.

I'd first met Rosie in a welding workshop at the Free Learning Centre in Footscray about two years ago. I was working on a long metal bar that was supposed to sit horizontally against the wall, to be used as railing for the steps leading up to my front door. Unfortunately, I was starting from zero when it came to the sorts of practical skills that went into making things and I had a bad habit of retaining almost nothing in classroom settings. I met Rosie the first day that our instructors let us into the workshop. I don't remember exactly what I was doing, but it must have been dangerous because Rosie filled my vision, saying, 'Are you alright?' Then the instructor came over to do a safety demonstration, using me as an example of what not to do, and I didn't see her again until three months ago, when she came into the Dan O'Conner Hotel. It took me a moment to recognise her as she walked up to the bar. She had her hair at chin level instead of the buzz cut she sported while we were attending classes together.

'You're that guy,' she said.

I gestured at the bar and shrugged, as if to say 'yeah'.

'Good to see that you still have your limbs.'

She was my only customer this late on a Tuesday. I found it easy to lean against the bar and talk shit with her. We had some surprising things in common: She was also the child of a second-generation migrant father (Somali in my case and Chinese Malaysian in her case) and a white mother. We were both fluent in Auslan and were learning Indonesian on Duolingo. She had the same opinions as I did about alternative education models and lifelong learning. She'd moved into an apartment around the corner on Carpenter Street and had just finished unpacking when she dropped in for a pint.

'I live so close to here it's ridiculous,' she said, and then asked me what time I finished work. I found myself confused by her question. I told her that I was going straight home. She said, 'Okay,' very slowly, and then left. She didn't look back as she walked away. I picked up her empty pint glass and took it to the rack. I felt embarrassed and guilty and foolish all at once.

Jackie walked over from the other bar. 'Who's she?' she asked. She was wearing a loose and ripped t-shirt, which looked worn but new at the same time. Earlier that night Jackie had told me that she was considering getting a septum piercing. I tried to imagine her with it and realised that I was staring at her nose as I spoke to her.

'She just moved around the corner,' I said.

'Oh wow, she must be loaded.'

The thought hadn't occurred to me at all, but now that Jackie mentioned it, it was a pretty expensive area and Rosie said she lived alone. 'I'm going on my break,' I said to Jackie and picked up my jacket from the basket under the bar. I began to walk away and then stopped and turned around. 'I think you could totally pull off a septum piercing.'

'I know, right?'

I walked past the toilets and into the kitchen. I found Ramesh drying his hands over a sink. 'Bro, do you reckon you can hook us up with a quick sandwich?' I asked him.

Ramesh looked around theatrically. 'Sure, we've just about closed the kitchen. Let's chill out back for a bit.' He beckoned me over, and I hovered over him as he made a lettuce, tomato and cheese sandwich and cut it into two triangular slices. I took one slice and he took the other and we walked out into the back door of the pub. As we passed Don's office, I spotted him asleep at his desk, his face covered by a copy of *The Age* newspaper. There was a new calendar on the wall above his desk – it was bright blue and featured pictures of Greek islands.

We sat on upturned milk crates and faced the bins as we ate. As usual, Ramesh quickly demolished his sandwich-half and lit a cigarette. I lingered over mine, forcing myself to slow down as I ate. I was following the instructions on a mindfulness app I'd downloaded a few weeks ago, and on the app's advice I had started eating slower, or, as the app called it, 'Eating Consciously'. When I was done Ramesh offered me a cigarette and I declined. I pulled out my notebook from my jacket pocket and unclipped the attached pen. I wrote down the word *Okay* in my notebook and then *Rosie doesn't look backwards.* Underneath in red pen was → *strata/littoral*, which I'd written a few days ago while watching a documentary on rock formation.

'What's that?' Ramesh asked.

'I'm just writing things down.'

Ramesh waved his hand in dismissal. 'Nah man. Me? I don't write anything down. I keep everything in here,' he said, pointing at his temple. He took a shallow drag of his cigarette and exhaled. 'Three people can only keep a secret if two of them are dead.'

Ramesh was older than me by almost two decades. We came from vastly different backgrounds but we had an understanding that transcended age. He would talk to me about his childhood in Mumbai as the youngest son of a rickshaw driver, and I would tell him about Julie, the forty-year-old woman I dated when I was seventeen, who taught me how to do my taxes online. The agreement was this: Ramesh would say something, and I would nod and agree with him. And then I would tell him something and he would say, 'That's just how it is, I'm afraid.' He had a rare gnomic quality to him, hugely expressive eyes, and sagging – almost Nixonian – jowls that trembled when he spoke.

'Yeah, I feel you,' I said, and I thanked him for the sandwich.

'Not a worry in the world,' he said.

After work, I went home and attempted to edit a poem. I was deleting and un-deleting the word *littoral* over and over before I finally gave up and went to bed, but not before I fished my notebook out of my jeans and took another look at the word *Okay*, and the arrow shape next to the words *strata/littoral.* Could a shape contain a whole poem? I didn't know.

A couple of days later Rosie came by the pub with three blonde white women who looked like they came from a religious-cult movie set on a horse farm. They were all wearing expensive boots and light-denim skirts and unbleached linen shirts and had their hair in simple and practical braids. They came to the bar as one, and the tallest woman said, 'Oh, I really do love Melbourne pubs.'

Rosie stuck her tongue out at me.

'Hey Rosie,' I said.

'Fancy meeting you here,' she said.

One of the women laughed, her teeth looking bright against her deep tan. 'You just moved here and you already know your local bartender!'

Rosie shrugged. 'I'm a nice person. People like me.'

Later, when she came up to the bar on her own, I asked her if she wanted to hang out sometime and she said, 'Sure. We can hang out sometime.' Her eyes were incredibly dark brown, almost black. It made her gaze knife-like. I added that to the list of things about her that I was noticing.

We didn't see each other again for almost two weeks. Rosie was performing in a play that was showing at La Mamma, and the lead-up to the opening night was filled with rehearsals. The play was a satire, the script a verbatim reproduction of an infamous *Q&A* episode that aired during the Sea Wall vote. Rosie was playing the Member for Gellibrand, Kaitlin Wu, whose famous speech railing against the proposed bill made her a brief star on the internet and whose spectacular fall from grace due to a plagiarism scandal during her career as a reporter was the subject of a Palme d'Or–winning documentary.

After the final dress rehearsal for the play, Rosie invited me to a bar in Fitzroy. I spent an age trying to pick my outfit and ended up going with a black coat and black jeans along with a white t-shirt that said 'die wall on it die' in the same font as the masthead of the German news magazine *Der Spiegel*. I regretted my choice as soon as I got on the tram at Flinders Street Station. I saw myself as others saw me: assimilating the grotesque and turning it into wearable art. What was I saying? I never knew. That was my problem. I found the bar, but the door was harder to find. I had to curl myself around a giant potted fern to get to it. Rosie spotted me as soon as I walked in and introduced me to a friend who was with her. Noelle was a producer for the theatre company that was putting on the play. I recognised her from the pub; she was the tall woman who just moved here from Sydney and was still enamoured by Melbourne's relatively cleaner air and dying pubs. Rosie and Noelle knew each other well. I learned that they'd come up together in the theatre scene in Sydney.

Their conversation about the results of 'the latest Resources Council four-year arts funding round' was beyond me and Rosie must have noticed my silence because she turned to me suddenly and said, 'I know exactly which emoji I am.' The warmth in her tone threw me off. It was as if she was revisiting an old conversation that we never had.

Rosie poured me a glass from a jug. The part of me that was a bartender noticed immediately that she exclusively preferred pale ales. I took a sip and considered showing off and saying, 'Is this a Morbid Towers Pale Ale?' but dismissed it. I didn't want to resort to cheap tricks to impress her.

'Does everyone have an emoji?' I asked.

'Absolutely. Everyone has one,' said Rosie. She was sure, and I felt compelled to believe her. The bar was dimly lit and the lights hung low, suspended from the ceiling by chain and wire. The booth we were in was built around a square table on three sides. Our drinks were served in white and black and red porcelain. According to Noelle, who'd asked the bartender all about them, they were pocked with blemishes formed during a traditional manufacturing process hundreds of years old. 'Aren't they lovely? They're from Japan!' she said. The warm light reflected brilliantly off the porcelain. It reminded me of a moment from a Jun'ichirō Tanizaki essay on light – he was writing about the specific interaction between warm, low light and porcelain bowls.

The light penetrates the superficial layers of the porcelain and scatters in the sub-surface layers, causing all the colours, but particularly red, to attain a deep brilliance.

'I'm definitely the sneezing face emoji,' said Noelle. 'My sinuses are a menagerie.'

'That's the Sydney leaving your body,' Rosie replied, and then immediately added, 'Sorry. That's a bad joke.' For a moment, there was a familiar and wretched silence as we considered the ramifications of the continent's forest cover being turned to particles that shred the membranes of our lungs.

Rosie broke the silence. 'I've decided I'm the smiley face with the cowboy hat.'

'I can see that,' I said.

'I know, right?'

'I have an Akubra at home and you'd definitely pull it off better than I can,' said Noelle.

'I wonder what mine is?' I asked. Rosie didn't respond but later that evening, after we'd all said goodbye and I was on the train home, she sent me a message that consisted of an upside-down smiling face emoji. The message made me silly with joy. I'm drunk, I thought. When was the last time I was drunk? It must have been over a year ago, at Sam's thirtieth.

I decided to go to the café at the end of my street before heading over to Sam's. I saw Chris outside the café, refilling a dog bowl with water. The other week, Chris told me that she'd be moving to Darwin when she finished her degree. I'd since been making extra effort to stop by the café and chat with her on the days she was there. She'd been working at the café for four years, the entire time I lived on Hyde Street, and I found myself preparing to miss her and wishing she'd stay. Even a small thing like my favourite barista moving to Darwin was enough to expose any sense of equilibrium for what it was: a fragile, treacherous moment that leaves you in its wake.

Next to the bowl was a puppy that looked like it was at least part Staffy. Its owner was admonishing it pre-emptively. 'Wait till the lady fills the bowl,' he said to the dog, which did not move and gave no indication that it had heard him. Meteor had skewed my perception of normal dog behaviour – I half expected the puppy to suddenly shoot off into the distance.

'He's so well behaved,' said Chris as she scratched it behind the ear.

'He forgets himself sometimes,' said the owner. As soon as Chris finished filling up the bowl, the puppy dove into it, sending some of the water flying out. Chris laughed brightly and wiped her hands off on her apron. The grass outside the café was dotted with red and yellow leaves. It was a glowing day and the water droplets shimmered in their flight. The night before, I had been sitting at a bar and telling a friend of mine about an essay I had read about trees, and she said that Bertolt Brecht only mentioned trees a few times in his poetry. 'What times are these,' he wrote in one poem about Germany in the 1930s, 'when a conversation about trees is almost a crime?' I felt that to locate joy in a moment was such a necessary thing. Chris's laughter was bright, and her voice broke at its high register. The light was brilliant, visible as striations between the branches of trees, the low morning sunlight scattered by the faint ever-present smog in the air.

Chris greeted me warmly as I approached and ushered me inside. It was just after the early morning rush, and the café was empty except for three white men with matching Border Force lanyards at the big table having a meeting, and the man and his dog outside. She began making my coffee and sent my order through to the kitchen. Then she told me about her plans for the weekend. 'My folks have a place near Cape Otway. I love the drive out there, especially at night. They want to sell the place before the next fire season, so this weekend is probably going to be the last time we can get out there.'

'Do you reckon they'd find a seller?' I didn't know much about the rich people housing market, but even I had heard of the forecasts and predictions over the next few years. Whole swathes of the countryside would soon be rendered uninhabitable, with no water and bushfires all year round.

'I don't know,' she said.

'I'm sorry you'll miss it.'

'Yeah, me too. It's my favourite place. That house is so full of memories,' she said. My Cuban sandwich with extra pickles arrived, and she placed it in a brown paper bag. I had gotten the same one every time for years. My consistency continuously delighted Chris.

'Cuban with extra pickles,' said Chris, handing it to me. I thanked her, and she said, 'Easy goings!' which was new. A few weeks ago, she had greeted me with a kiss on the cheek, and that also was new. Chris was forever trying new greetings and goodbyes because she got bored of saying the same things over and over, as she once explained to me. It was an aspect of her personality that I had started incorporating into my own life. The other day I said, 'Hiya!' to a customer and it was thrilling.

As I left the café, I had an urge to text Rosie. I'm becoming bold. I got to my car and sat inside for a few minutes, thinking it over. Rosie once told me about a theory she had. According to her, it is possible to imbue an unsent text message with such energy that the person who it is meant for will feel that you are communicating with them directly, even if the content itself never reaches them. After several minutes of thinking about it, I texted her, 'Howdy,' along with a cowboy face emoji.

Sam's place was a mess. There were empty pizza boxes and mugs with curdling tea in them all over the living room. Sam himself looked very tired: his eyes were ringed and he looked like he hadn't shaved in days. On the coffee table was an unopened Amazon box, presumably containing a new kind of dog food.

'Meteor sends his apologies that he can't be here to greet you himself but, you know ...'

I looked around Sam's living room, relishing the freedom to just stand still. Ever since Meteor entered Sam's life, I'd stopped coming over as often to his small one-bedroom apartment. Whereas before his apartment seemed spacious to me, these days it was a cramped battleground. Meteor would immediately crash into me and begin barking whenever I entered. Sam insisted that Meteor loved me and was only excited to see me, but sometimes it felt like Meteor saw me as a threat to his relationship with Sam. At work, Jackie thought I was jealous of Meteor replacing me in Sam's affections, while Ramesh thought that Meteor previously had racist owners. Sam was oblivious to this, which annoyed me, but I was also aware of how happy Meteor had made my best friend. The dog had given him purpose and structure – they seemed to share a bond that I couldn't understand, having never owned a pet.

Sam led me to the bedroom where Meteor was bundled up in thick blankets. I peered closely at the dog. 'How long have you been trying to eat bottle caps?' I said to Meteor.

'He just loves them, doesn't he?' Sam said. He brushed past me to smother Meteor in kisses and scratches. Meteor seemed to be grateful for the attention, and he seized up dramatically as he moaned, leading Sam to seize up as well out of sympathy.

'The poor thing,' said Sam. He looked like he hadn't showered in days. His apartment had a stale and heavy smell, as if he hadn't opened a window in days either.

I approached Meteor and he stirred, picking up his head. He stared at me out of one baleful eye, like he was calculating devious attack strategies.

'I'm sorry you're so sick,' I said to him. Meteor moaned in response.

Sam picked up one of Meteor's front paws and mimed a regal wave, 'Thank you for coming to visit me.'

'My pleasure,' I said to the dog.

Meteor had his head on Sam's lap as I drove us to the vet. He seemed more alert now that we were on the move. I was suddenly feeling guilty for dawdling so long at the café.

I didn't know it was serious. I told Sam and he waved my apology away.

'It's my fault, really. I didn't want to bother you by making you rush over to mine,' he said.

'Cool beans.'

'Cool beans?' Sam raised an eyebrow, waiting for an answer.

'People say it.'

'People say it?'

'Rosie says it.'

'Rosie? I've never heard of anyone with that name. Is she a friend of yours?' said Sam, his voice incredulous. I snuck a glance at Meteor, who hadn't understood a word of what we were saying. He looked uncomfortable and unhappy about it. I felt for him strongly in that moment.

They wouldn't let me into the patient room – the nurse in charge gave me an arch look and pointed her pen at a sign beside the corridor that said, 'STAFF, PETS, AND OWNERS ONLY. NO VISITORS,' which stopped me cold in my tracks. I loitered outside the clinic front door and was overcome by a familiar and deep longing for a cigarette. I welcomed the craving like an old friend, along with its tension and distraction. I had quit smoking three years ago when the price of a twenty-pack of smokes tripled. Not to mention, I had, around that time, discovered that my teeth were developing tobacco stains. My father had deeply stained teeth from a lifetime of smoking, and I had always promised myself that I'd get new teeth if mine ever got that bad. I had enjoyed cigarettes perhaps more than I did any other solitary activity, as much as I loved finishing a poem.

I found an outdoor bench and sat down and tried not to think about whether my career would fizzle out into nothing after the release of my promising, if scattered, first collection. After a few minutes the nurse who had barred my entry into the surgery earlier came out for a smoke break. She looked younger than me, in her early or mid-twenties. She sat down across from me and it occurred to me that I might be sitting in her favourite spot – I was shaded from the wind by the broad leafy oak that dominated the small park beside the vet, and the edges of its branches cast a cool shade over the seat, unlike the seats across from me, which were bathed in the full light of the sun.

'Are you with the beagle?' she called out to me.

'Yes, Meteor, that's my friend's beagle,' I said.

'Cute little guy.' She was smoking a Chinese brand of imported cigarettes, and it smelled like it might be harsh.

'Can I bum a smoke?' I asked. She finished her break and stood up, handing me one as she walked past me and went back inside. I brought the cigarette to my mouth before I realised that I didn't have a lighter. I suddenly felt foolish and stuffed it in my front pocket, where it stuck out the top like a pen.

Sam eventually came outside. 'I didn't know you started smoking again,' he said, spotting the cigarette in my top pocket. I shrugged. Sam had always hated my smoking habit and had been trying to get me to quit for years. He also never stopped inviting me to his weekly pickup basketball games in North Melbourne even though I had never taken him up on the offer.

'How's Meteor?' I asked.

Sam exhaled deeply. 'Yeah, turns out he ate three bottle caps, not one. They want to keep him overnight for observation to see if he passes some of the bottle caps on his own.'

'Poor little guy. I feel sorry for him,' I said.

'Me too,' he said. The veterinarian told Sam that there was nothing to do until Meteor tried to take a shit, so we should just come back tomorrow. Since we were in Yarraville, we decided to head to the park and gawk at part of a massive gate they were building in the former dockyards. Huge blocks of stone waiting to be shipped to offshore construction platforms formed massive blocks and pyramids on the yards, where shipping containers were once stacked just as high. We found a nice spot that gave us a good view of the construction site. Of course, you couldn't see the whole structure. It was just too large to fit into a human's perspective. In fact, it took a considerable amount of mental gymnastics to realise that the massive altar of criss-crossing steel that filled our vision across the river was in fact a small corner of the portcullis.

'I still don't understand how they get that thing all the way out into the middle of the ocean,' said Sam.

'I think they float it out there,' I said.

We sat in silence for a while, watching the cranes and trucks moving blocks of stone around. Eventually Sam asked me to drop him back home. On the way, he said, 'Look. Congrats on the book. I'm really stoked for you and your poetry is going to blow everyone away. I'm sorry if I didn't communicate that earlier.' I wanted to hug him, but I didn't want to accidentally crash and kill the two of us, so I tightened my grip on the steering wheel and renewed my attention on the road.

'Thank you,' I said. 'Sorry about this thing with Meteor.'

'What can you do?' said Sam.

By the time I got home, I only had enough time to watch two episodes of *Knives in Siberia* before I had to shower and get ready for work. It was mid-afternoon and the sun was brilliant, casting long and low shadows. I elected to walk to work and by the time I arrived, fifteen minutes early, I was feeling unusually energised. The happy hour crowd from the tech firm across the street was just beginning to trickle in. Their company was currently trialling a four-day working week, which meant that on Thursdays they had the whole place to themselves, and after-work drinks became a ritual for them. In the back office, Don was hunched over the ancient computer he used to run the pub. I greeted him as I passed to get to the lockers. 'Is Jackie here yet?' he said without turning away from the dense Excel spreadsheet on his screen.

'I only just got here,' I said. Don grunted and turned back to the computer screen. After I stowed my bag and coat in my locker, I went through the kitchen on my way to the bar. Ramesh was leaning against the sliding door to the fridge.

'Chef's not here yet,' he said.

'Again? What happened to Mohammed?' I asked.

Ramesh shrugged. 'No idea. He just stopped showing up,' he said.

'Is Jackie here yet?'

'I haven't seen her.'

I peered through the hallway and into the bar. It looked busy and I wasn't on for at least another fifteen minutes. I had nothing better to do so I followed Ramesh out into the back courtyard and we sat on the milk crates facing the bins.

'The kitchen staff all think he was taken by the police,' said Ramesh.

'Is there any way to find out if he was?'

'Hard to know anything without getting involved.'

I finished work at close to 1am. Rosie had texted me earlier that evening asking if I wanted to go to a party in Brunswick East with her, but I told her I was working. *What time do u finish?* she replied. I told her the time, and she didn't respond for hours. At close to midnight, I got a text from her saying, *drink + boogie at rope factory?* and then, a half hour later, *Went to sleep! xxx.* The exchange left me feeling stretched out and relieved. Don was in a bad mood due to Mohammed's absence, and the kitchen service was terrible all night. I could hear Don in the back saying, 'Not good enough!' to the kitchen staff. I felt bad for Ramesh, who was forced to do Mohammed's job and his own in the kitchen. Jackie was insistent that the police took Mohammed and she told us about a series of raids the police were conducting all over Melbourne that week. Her story was backed up by the fact that Ramesh claimed to have heard sirens all night the past few evenings. I was inclined to believe her. As the only Indigenous person at work, we all assumed she knew more than us about these things. It was common knowledge that Indigenous people had their own secret internet that ran on a parallel infrastructure, so she was the one we all turned to whenever we heard a new rumour.

'It is almost certainly because of the Exclusion Act,' Ramesh said, when he came over to the bar for a knockoff.

It was almost closing time and Jackie and Don were counting the money in the registers as I reset the bar. As soon as Ramesh mentioned the EA, it was as if the air in the room soured and we were suddenly bored by the whole discussion. Don finished up the count at his register, and looked around, 'Why are you lot still here?'

I asked Jackie if she could drop me off at home. 'Sure,' she said, and I followed her to the car park. Her black Civic was in the same spot it always was, to the left of a broad plane tree.

'I heard you have a book coming out,' said Jackie as we got in the car.

'Yeah, it's a small collection of poems,' I said.

'What's it called?'

'*List of Known Remedies*.'

'Remedies to what?'

'I don't know,' I said. And I thought for a moment and spoke again. 'It's about shame, and guilt, and intractable problems inherent to living.'

'Ah,' said Jackie.

'That's what a review that came out the other day said it was about,' I said.

'I like the word "intractable". It feels nice, even though its meaning isn't,' said Jackie.

'You're right. In-tract-able,' I said.

'In … tra … ctaaaable,' Jackie said, before giggling. We'd stopped at a red light on Dynon Road. Ahead of us was a van covered in a thick layer of dust. Someone had scribbled 'fuck' with their finger on the back window. 'I feel like I get drunk around you guys, even though I'm not drinking anymore.'

'How is it?'

'It's boring, but I feel good about it,' she said. I found it strange how Jackie was so talkative and easygoing outside of work, but so serious and quiet when on the clock. When we pulled over in front of my house, I turned to her and asked, 'Do you really think the police took him?'

Jackie took a deep breath and said, 'Fucked if I know, hey. They do it on purpose, don't they? They make it so we can never really know for sure.' I didn't know what to say. I felt a knot forming in my stomach. What was there to say?

'Are you working tomorrow?'

'Nah, I've got tomorrow off. I was thinking of getting my piercing done tomorrow,' she said.

I was at my door when Sam called me. I picked up while juggling the keys with my other hand. 'Hey mate.'

'I can't sleep,' said Sam. 'I need to know he'll be okay; I just need to know he'll be fine.'

'I'm sure he'll be fine. Meteor is a champ.'

'He's a goddamn champion. He's so good.'

'Have you eaten at all?'

'Not really.'

'Can you do that, please? And drink a lot of water? And then go to sleep? Please?'

The next day, I went over to Sam's place at around noon. The door was open and I let myself in. Sam was in the kitchen eating cereal and watching the news. There was an accident on one of the offshore platforms constructing the sea wall and seven contractors were dead. The prime minister was on the news visiting the families of the deceased. He was surrounded by large and square-faced men in uniforms, their chests glittering with medals, as he awkwardly forced a grieving widow to shake his hand. As the reporter spoke, the news ticker updated the running tally of fatal accidents on the construction platforms, as well as providing updated casualty figures for an air strike that had accidentally hit a school bus near Lahore, as well as showing the latest run tally from the cricket. Sam turned off the TV and greeted me warmly. He looked transformed. He had shaved and was wearing a clean shirt and seemed in much better spirits than he had been the other day. His place was still a mess though, with empty cups and plates and takeaway packaging all around. 'Do you want some cornflakes?' he said.

'I just ate.'

'The vet just called. Meteor passed all the bottle caps with no problems at all.'

The nurse from the other day wasn't working when we arrived, and I managed to follow Sam into the vet's office. The vet, a rather weedy-looking white guy with thick, round glasses, was effusive in his praise of Meteor. 'He's a real trooper. We thought we'd need to surgically intervene,' he said. Meteor was at Sam's feet, watching us discuss him. Sam was crouched down, rubbing his side. I reached over cautiously to scratch Meteor behind the ear and he surprised me by leaning into my hand.

'You must feel so cooped up! Let's get you to the park,' Sam said to Meteor, talking to him in a baby voice. As we approached Yarraville Park, Meteor took off towards the grass and Sam ran off after him. Rosie texted me telling me she'd taken the day off and asking if I wanted to grab a beer. I replied immediately saying, *Yes please. I'd like that a lot.* Across the river, a huge crane turned, lifting a massive steel beam into the air. I watched it spin slowly in the wind, suspended in the air by a thin film of wire about as thick as my forearm. Meteor tackled Sam to the ground and they both rolled around in the grass, laughing and yapping.

The East
Australia Company
Mango Bridge

Roanna Gonsalves

A long, long time ago, the East Australia Company Mango Bridge did not exist. It is hard to believe but it is true. The Gadigal used their canoes to cross the water between Sydney Cove and Kirribilli. But the European convicts, the Asiatic servants, the Maori princesses, the Shanghai sailors and the Boston veterans had to travel up river and rely on Mister Blue's boat. Once they got to the other side, they had to walk all the way to their destinations, or pay good coin to ride on sick, slow horses rejected by the military. Even on an impeccable day, without the usual hordes on the shores trying to get away from family disputes or failed arrangements of one kind or another, it could still take a very long time.

Everything changed in the year 1814. Shammy and Maree had a series of realisations. Then they made the East Australia Company Mango Bridge. This is the story of how it happened.

In the time of Cora Gooseberry and Bungaree, just after the time of Patyegarang and Pemulwuy and Bennelong, there was a tree that drank from the heart of this land. But Shammy was not yet interested in it. She was more interested in the British military officers, magistrates, and judges in the colony who considered themselves to be poets. Such persons were always invited to the dinners hosted by Governor Macquarie. Shammy knew this for she was often called upon to serve them her special duck curry and, as she cleaned up after them, to hear the 'Recitation of the Odes'. These odes brimmed with unadulterated praise of the natural and the unnatural alike, in verse that was best described, if one were to exert some Christian charity, as deserving of Christian forgiveness. Shammy knew that the Bards of Sydney Cove, as she called them under her breath, would succumb to one or all of the seven deadly sins, and prolong the 'Recitation of the Odes' for as long as they could in the presence of the Governor. In doing so, they would keep the colony's printer, Mister Howe, in their company and away from the printing office until daybreak. Shammy was counting on such history repeating itself on Friday night, the seventeenth of June, 1814. This was not for the enhancement of the global store of the literary arts. It was to protect the East Australia Company, the underground business that she co-owned with the Gadigal-Goan Maree.

Shammy was employed as a servant of Mister and Mrs Ritchie. But her second official job was as Mister Howe's assistant compositor. That Friday, he had already supervised Shammy as she finished compositing the front page of the *Sydney Gazette*, with text approved by the Governor's secretary. Mister Howe had then entrusted her with the printing of fifty copies, to be ready for distribution the next day. Shammy would be sure to do this, just not in the way that Mister Howe was expecting.

That month, Shammy and her business partner Maree had been busy coordinating the daily but covert operations of the East Australia Company or EAC. It took time and patience to ensure high standards in the production and packaging of the latest consignment of EAC pashmina shawls and monkey caps. These products were made from the finest hair of the Blue Mountains goats. The pashmina shawls and monkey caps, or Templar caps as the memsahibs called them, were exported to the lucrative market of the Bengal Presidency, which was full of middle-men who yoked the aspirations of the Asiatic natives to the hunger of the East India Company. These native but rich Asiatics shrank at the first sign of winter, emerging only to eat Darjeeling oranges. Pashmina shawls were a luxury item. Monkey caps were a necessity. Shammy had spread a rumour that an EAC pashmina shawl and monkey cap would be worn by the Prince Regent at his coronation, upon the death of his mad father, any day now. This made the EAC pashmina shawls and monkey caps the only winter accessories that the native but rich Asiatics would be seen wearing in public. It increased demand to such an extent that the backorder was two years long.

By the Thursday of that week, Shammy and Maree got word that the workers at the EAC workshop deep in the Blue Mountains had packed all the pashmina shawls and monkey caps into a large box. The box would be taken from that subterranean facility to the shores of Sydney Cove by a chain of porters working the Friday night shift. It would be deposited in a secure location known only to Maree. She would pick it up and then, with Shammy's help, deliver it into the hands of Bhavani, an artist and professional sailor, hiding in the mangroves. Shammy planned to deliver it to Bhavani after she finished work at the printing office. Bhavani would secretly transport the box to Kirribilli, then to a sturdy East Indiaman bound for Calcutta the next week. The lascars at every step of the journey had already been generously compensated to ensure loyalty. Yes of course, the core EAC business of raising the mountain goats, shearing them, weaving pashmina shawls and monkey caps and transporting them had to be done in secret, away from the ruthless eyes of the Macarthurs in Sydney and the East India Company in Bengal. This was not impossible.

Maree told Shammy that her father was from Salvador Do Mundo, Goa. He was broad of shoulder but unreliable. He stuck around while his sahib served the previous two governors. Then he left Parramatta one winter afternoon, running all the way to Sydney, to get on a ship bound for

Shanghai. Maree called and called his name. But he did not look back, not even once. He had left her with nothing but a mango seed and an oily forehead. 'Pai, pai,' she wept in the shade of a grumpy tree, rubbing the seed, a Mankurad mango seed brought all the way from Goa, as her father receded from her memory and into her imagination. In answer, all she got was a shower of tired wattle falling upon her like curses, yellow curses sticking in her hair. Maree threw the mango seed into the ground and stomped on it with the force of a betrayed daughter. Then she turned to her aunty, who convinced her to make the most of this dual inheritance, of mango seed and oily forehead. Maree knew not how until the day she met Shammy fresh off the *Queen Anne* from Bombay.

Shammy had arrived with her sahib and memsahib, the almost aristocratic and completely industrious Ritchies, a childless couple who had made their wealth in opium, slaves and tea. They never ceased to inform anyone who would listen that they were cousins to William Ritchie of Edinburgh. Shammy had an oily forehead too. It was the result of the daily massaging of coconut oil into her hair. She wanted to style it in the manner of her idol, the great Mary Wollstonecraft herself.

Shammy may have come across as a demure servant in public, nodding to please at every opportunity. She may have exaggerated when she told her sahib's friends that her duck curry recipe had been passed on to her through seven generations of her mother's family. She may have pretended to be an expert in Vedic astronomy when called upon to tell the fortunes of the Europeans. But in actual fact she was a financial mastermind, possibly born of Marwari blood, in the image and likeness of a Jagat Seth, former financiers to an empire. Shammy was barely interested in Maree being Goan. She was more interested in Maree being Gadigal, more interested in her vast network, on her mother's side, of sisters, brothers, aunties, uncles, cousins and friends spread beyond the reach of the Europeans. When Shammy first arrived in Sydney, she brought along with her four Kashmiri goats. The first and fattest goat was used for Christmas dinner that year. The second was used for the Prince Regent's birthday celebrations. Shammy had plans for the third and the fourth goats. With Maree's help she released them into the area near Kedumba, long before the Europeans made a big fuss about their first crossing of The Mountains. The Kedumba air proved to be an unusually fecund gift. The two goats turned into eight and then eight hundred in the span of a few months, their hair finer than that of their Kashmiri ancestors. Maree and her cousins turned out to be born weavers, blessed with the fingers of the gods. With the right equipment that Shammy procured through unchristian favours at the Commissary, they soon began to shear the goats, and weave their fine hair into intricate designs on the East Australia

Company's premium range of pashmina shawls. The monkey caps didn't require as much skill. Shammy entrusted them to the teenaged children of the weavers. She only tolerated Maree and cultivated a friendship with her, exploiting Maree's desire to find out more about her Goan heritage, so she could expand the EAC. But it was risky.

The shooting of the natives by the settlers had become a common indulgence, undertaken with impunity for many years. The EAC were losing important workers more quickly than Shammy and Maree could replace them. Recruitment, training, the building of trust, all this took time. The fact that Shammy had to work in her day jobs as a servant of the Ritchies and as an assistant compositor to Mister Howe slowed down the recruitment process considerably. It added to the risk. Shammy needed to act decisively if the business were to meet demand and fulfil her greater ambitions.

So, through her network of servants in Sydney and Parramatta, which was inextricably connected with the network of the sahibs and memsahibs, she began to spread rumours of a race of native warrior tribes, not unlike the Mongols, who roamed the interior, and had been armed by China. They were not only depraved but also pagan. Disembowelment, decapitation, offerings of virgin blood to the antipodean equivalent of Satan, nothing was beyond them. They even had links to the ferment in France, old and new. Despite the immediate effectiveness of this scheme, Shammy knew this was only a temporary insurance against further exploration by the settlers. She set to thinking about more permanent determent, with the full force of British Law backing it up. She found it, or to be more accurate, it was thrust upon her, on Thursday afternoon, while working at her second official job as Mister Howe's assistant compositor.

At first Shammy didn't realise the extent of the opportunity when Mister Howe spoke to her.

'Shammy, I wish I could avoid it, but I have to be present at the Governor's dinner tomorrow.'

'Must you really go?'

'Oh yes, I must. If I want to flatter the Governor into getting us the new printing press.'

'Good luck, Mister Howe.'

'I would be very grateful if you took care of the printing for me. It's only the first page. Fifty copies.'

'I'm honoured that you would trust me, Mister Howe.'

'I will have to suffer through the "Recitation of the Odes".'

'You'll get through them, Mister Howe.'

'Make sure you hang up each new copy properly. It won't do to have a wet *Sydney Gazette*.'

'I won't fold them until they are as dry as Bligh.'

'Oh Shammy, you're a dangerous one.'

'You can rely on me, Mister Howe.'

'I know I can, Shammy, I know I can.'

That Thursday night, when she met Maree as usual under the unending aerial roots of the Birra Birra trees by the water's edge, she mentioned in passing that Mister Howe would not be supervising her printing of the *Sydney Gazette*.

'I'm going to print a notice about the EAC in the extra space on the first page, down at the bottom, let more people know that they can purchase our goods from the store behind Mrs Reiby's establishment.'

'Mister Howe won't be there?'

'No. I just told you that.'

'And the Governor has already signed the order?'

'We don't need further approval, if that's what you're asking.'

'Then you're stupid to waste the opportunity on an advertisement.'

'I was educated by the great Mary Wollstonecraft herself.'

'If by educated you mean you read aloud *A Vindication of the Rights of Woman* to your memsahib every day for ten years, then I was educated by Shakespeare himself.'

'You're so difficult,' Shammy said to Maree.

'You're not the easiest, either. I'm only here because of my people.'

'"Your people"? Or to get as much information as you can from me about Goa?'

'You're here to get as much information as you can from me about my mother's family so you can have an unlimited supply of workers.'

'We can have an unlimited supply of workers.'

'I still maintain that you're stupid.'

'If you're so smart, what do you think we should do?'

'I'll tell you when I see the proofs.'

That Friday evening in June, Shammy and Maree could have completed their task by midnight and made it in time to pick up the box of EAC pashmina shawls and monkey caps from the secret location and deliver it to Bhavani by midnight. All they had to do was to print fifty copies of the *Sydney Gazette*, hang them to dry and fold them in preparation for next morning's distribution. But only five minutes after they entered the printery, lit the candles, and began to read the approved text that had already been composed, Shammy began to roll her tongue around her teeth, making sucking, cheeping noises.

'Stop that,' Maree said.

'I have a piece of duck stuck in my back teeth,' said Shammy.

'You taught me to cook curry and my profit on it is I know how to curse you with it. The plague rid you for learning me your curry recipe.'

Shammy hated it when Maree modified Shakespeare to fit the circumstances. It reminded Shammy of the holes in her own soul. Maree was Patyegarang's niece's niece on her mother's side, and had grown up with her aunty's aunty reading Mister Dawes' copy of *The Tempest* aloud to her. Shammy had been told this a hundred times, whenever she expressed the slightest displeasure. Had Maree been Madhoo or Jummah, Shammy would not have hesitated in putting her in her place. But Maree, with her vast network on her mother's side, of sisters, brothers, aunties, uncles, cousins and friends, spread beyond the imagination of the sahibs, was too valuable to her.

Maree finished reading the text of the Governor's Order. The heat from the candles made her forehead more oily. She looked directly at Shammy.

'This Order makes our people seem to be what they are not.'

Maree's ponderous attention to sentences and their unspoken meaning impeded the agility of the EAC. It was one of the perils of doing business with her. Shammy wished to finish the printing quickly and then attend to the more important delivery of the premium EAC pashmina shawls and monkey caps. But she said nothing. She let Maree continue.

'You would be stupid to waste such an opportunity on a risky advertisement when you could do so much more.'

Shammy felt obliged to ask as expected, 'Why risky?'

'Do you want to attract the attention of the Macarthurs, the attention of the East India Company? The EAC is a mystery. Let's keep it that way.'

'What would you have us do?'

'The Order is cruel.'

'This is a cruel place.'

'Change the text,' said Maree.

Shammy was used to Maree's impertinence. But this was going a bit too far. She heard the wind whip about Macquarie Place and Bridge Street, unable to make up its mind.

'Not of the entire front page. Only of the Governor's Order. And not of the entire Order. Just the middle paragraphs, to minimise scrutiny.'

'But why?'

'So our people will have some reprieve from the shootings in Bringelly, in Airds. And also in Appin.'

Shammy saw the shadows leaping off the walls. She knew the terrible consequences for servants when they forgot their place.

'Impossible. The text has already been approved.'

'No one will find out.'

'Of course they will. When they read the *Gazette*.'

'No one will know it was us.'

'Mister Howe will know.'

'Does he really remember every front page of every *Sydney Gazette*?'

The grimy heat, the smell of soot, intensified in the printing office. Shammy saw her oily forehead reflected in Maree's own. She took a step back, as if recoiling, or perhaps making more space for the force of this vision.

Maree was such a hindrance, with her constant condescension, her egotistical quoting of Shakespeare, her unshakeable awareness that she was better than those around her. But Maree's network was indispensable. It suited Shammy that Maree's need to ensure the survival of her people was perfectly aligned with Shammy's business ambitions. Then she thought of Bhavani waiting in secret at Sydney Cove for the box of premium EAC pashmina shawls and monkey caps, risking his life.

'We don't have time for that. Bhavani leaves at midnight,' said Shammy.

'We would have had more time had we been able to take the box directly to Kirribilli ourselves.'

'But we can't. Unless you can get your beautiful Aunty Karoo to lend us her canoe.'

Shammy made sure to refer to Cora Gooseberry as 'your beautiful Aunty Karoo' whenever she spoke to Maree. She knew that a little flattery could oil the EAC's line of supply like nothing else.

'Aunty Karoo's canoes are not available tonight.'

'Then we can't change the text.'

Maree began to look more closely at the Governor's Order.

'Come up with other solutions,' she said. Then she walked to a window and opened it.

At that moment, a candle went out. Yet suddenly a new flame began to flicker in Shammy's mind. The printing office expanded as if inhaling the universe. Possibilities began to reveal themselves, some clearly, some still sheathed in uncertainty. Shammy looked around the room.

She saw the wooden printing press. It wore its age on its frame. But to her it was a breathing animal. It was through the very press before them that this continent was eaten and then spat out as a colony. It was here in this workshop that the smoke of *terra nullius*, no man's land, was solidified from a mere wish into government policy. It was here that orders were given for reprisals against individuals and communities. With charcoal, gum, and shark oil, as the printer worked the inkballs to distribute ink evenly across worn metal type, a colony was carved from a continent. The *Sydney Gazette* spread the stories of this colony across the world, through sail and through whisper, through a process of accretion and embellishment, through a process of sculpting and shaping according to the needs of those who controlled the purse. Shammy understood the power of this alchemy. She gripped the frame of the press tightly, felt the strength of the tree from which it had been cut.

Shammy was the fastest compositor in all of the colonies across the world. Mister Howe had said so himself on many an occasion. She would be a fool not to harness this reputation to reverse a process that was in motion, and yes, also to serve her own interests: in Parramatta, Van Diemen's Land, Norfolk Island, New Zealand, Otaheite, Shanghai, Calcutta, Madras, Bombay, St Kitts, Jamaica, Boston, London, the Isle of Mull, even in Edinburgh, where Shammy hoped her work would be noticed by William Ritchie himself. There was a rumour that he wanted to start a new daily paper in Scotland. Perhaps one day she would be a newspaperwoman, in charge of telling the colonies how to think.

As Shammy let this new understanding settle upon her, she felt again the piece of meat stuck in her grinder. She began making the tongue noises again. Shammy couldn't stop the tip of her tongue from seeking out the gap between her two back teeth and trying to dislodge the shred of duck meat wedged between them. She knew, from past experience, that if there was one thing that set Maree's nerves on edge, it was tongue against teeth. She could not afford to displease

Maree. But she could not stop her tongue from doing as it pleased either.

In an effort to dispel some of this energy, Shammy decided to demonstrate to Maree the inking of the type. The ink balls were made of soft wool covered with forgiving dog leather, non-porous and non-confrontational, doing as they were told, black with the ink they had spread on the type over the years. Without them there would be no *Sydney Gazette*. It was almost like kneading dough, making the ink submit to the will of the inker, making meaning from lampblack and oil, taking the detritus of a fire and refashioning it into indelible authority.

'It takes a lot of skill to distribute the ink evenly,' Shammy said, trying but failing to sound like a boss.

Maree looked up from the Governor's Order. There was a touch of precariousness in the way she held her head, as if she might turn and leave that very minute, if it pleased her. Shammy felt she must impress upon her stubborn, secretive business partner the urgency of the situation.

'If we miss Bhavani, we will have to wait another three months.'

'I am aware of that.'

'Mister Howe may return early too.'

'Not if the officers, magistrates, and judges keep reciting their odes.'

A pause.

Then Maree said, with the force of a sun setting irrevocably on a colony, 'This Order is dangerous to our people.'

After this truth, all Shammy could manage was the flimsiest of attempts at control.

'Your mother's people,' she said.

'Our workers,' her business partner replied.

Maree began to read the approved proofs of the Governor's Order aloud.

'THE GOVERNOR and COMMANDER IN CHIEF feels much Regret in having to advert to the unhappy Conflicts which have lately taken place between the Settlers in the remote Districts of Bringelly, Airds, and Appin, and the Natives of the Mountains adjoining those Districts; and He sincerely laments that any Cause should have been given on either Side for the sanguinary and cruel Acts which have been reciprocally perpetrated by each Party ... '

Maree stopped reading. 'It begins with such dangerous inaccuracy. The cruelty has not been reciprocally perpetrated.'

At times like this, Shammy wished that Maree would concern herself less with the meticulous analysis of every single word ever written in this world. This quest for signification was the surest road to ruin. She wished Maree's ferocity could be channelled towards improving the EAC supply line instead.

The approved Order had the usual dribs and drabs about the Governor feeling regret for the ongoing conflict between the settlers and Maree's people. Of course, the settlers always started it, as usual forcing their assumptions upon those not like them. Maree knew that. Shammy knew that. Everyone knew that. This time, Maree's cousins had helped themselves to some maize and other grain from a farm. And those settlers came crying like babies to the Governor.

Maree said, 'We have always taken from the land as is our need and we have always given back to the land, as is our responsibility.'

Shammy knew that Maree's interruptions would continue endlessly. She thought of Bhavani waiting for them. Maree continued reading.

'... *In such Circumstances it will be highly becoming and praise-worthy in the British Settlers to exercise their Patience and Forbearance, and therein to shew the Superiority they possess over those unenlightened Natives by adopting a conciliatory Line of Conduct towards them, and returning to the Performance of those friendly Offices by which they have so long preserved a good Understanding with them. In acting thus, they will reflect Credit on themselves, and most effectually secure their own personal Safety; but should Outrages be then further committed by the Natives, on*

Information being given to the Magistrate of the District, the most active Measures will be taken for the Apprehension and Punishment of the Aggressors, in like Manner as under similar Circumstances would take Place when British Subjects only were concerned.'

Maree stopped reading. 'It sounds like he's praising us but in truth he's appeasing the settlers. He says they are superior to us. He says we are unenlightened. There will be massacres to follow.'

Shammy didn't appreciate being the target of such condescension. She felt compelled to reach for an interesting segue, hoping its relevance would reveal itself in some way. But nothing came to mind. It was long past sunset. Time was running out. She felt an air of surrender rearrange the room. She brought out a quill and ink pot and motioned to Maree to lay the official Governor's Order on Mister Howe's desk nearby.

'What is the first sentence you want changed?'

There was thunder outside. Shammy wasn't sure if it was real or imagined because her tongue was at it again. That piece of meat was really getting unbearable. Shammy wanted to dig it out that very instant. She wished she could somehow sharpen the tip of her tongue so it could get into the gap between her teeth more easily.

Maree said, 'What confidence does it inspire when one is told that one's complaints of murder will be "duly attended to" as if they were requests for the purchase of Bengal soap?'

'Is that all you want changed?'

Shammy dipped her quill in the inkpot. She crossed out some words and scribbled other words across the approved text. Then, realising that she was quite enjoying the task of rewriting the Governor's Order, she worked on the text some more. She added new adjectives and adverbs. She took out a few others. When she was finished, she asked with a smug anticipation of praise, 'What do you think of this?'

Maree looked at the changed Governor's Order. She began to frown. Shammy, newly nervous at this scrutiny of her work, began to roll her tongue around her teeth. She felt pain. She imagined rot. She imagined blood and pus swirling in her mouth. Then she saw Maree looking at her and she stopped her noises. The wind blew in through the open window, bringing the desert to the coast. Shammy was grateful to the elements for conspiring with the EAC. The heat in the wind meant that the ink would dry quickly. They could finish the printing and the drying and the folding of the *Sydney Gazette* and still make it in time to deliver the box to Bhavani without much risk. She focused on the brass pot that held a set of quills. The light from the candles made them glow like compliments. She waited for Maree's response with an expectant tilt of her head, ready to be coy about any effusive admiration.

But Maree was unmoved.

'Is this the best you can do? The new Order must sound unequivocally supportive of my people.'

Shammy was a little disappointed by what she saw as Maree's inability to appreciate literary excellence. But this disappointment was overshadowed by her greater impulse to rise to the challenge that Maree had just thrown at her. She loved compositing. She loved the thrill of creating beauty with metal and ink, of being in charge of telling the reader how to think. She loved the challenge of rendering the spirit of the author's words on the page through the selection and placement of type. So when Maree wanted the new Order to sound more assertive, Shammy immediately reached for the upper-case type. Mister Howe had been making do with a shortage of lower-case type, that was true. Last month she had to composite a whole page only using upper-case before she found some lower-case letters at the back of the printing office. But that Friday night, the surplus of upper-case type offered immense, pleasurable possibilities. Shammy began to make corrections on the handwritten Order while at the same time playing around with the metal type in the galley, such was her skill.

She set to work so intently that she lost all sense of time and place, all sense of the EAC, all sense of Bhavani waiting for her, all sense of inhibition, all sense of bodily control. She may have passed wind. She may have dug the wax out of her ears. She may have finally managed to insert her tongue into the gap between her back teeth followed by a loud sucking noise. She was completely unaware of herself, deliciously lost in the twenty-six letters of the English language. It was only when Maree sighed with such irritation that another candle went out, and the room darkened considerably, that Shammy was jolted back into the present moment. She heard Maree say, 'Before you do anything to the text, I need to do something to your teeth.'

Maree looked around for an instrument with which to work on Shammy's grinder. The instrument most suitable to the task was another quill, sharp and reliable. She lifted it out of the brass pot and then began to feel around Shammy's skirt.

'What are you doing?'

'Looking for your box of turmeric.'

'But that's my turmeric,' Shammy said.

'All right,' Maree said, and stepped away.

The pain in her gums had intensified and Shammy was desperate for relief. So she stopped the compositing process and gave Maree her box with which to disinfect the quill. She opened her mouth wide and let Maree have her head. Maree began to read the changed text aloud as she worked on Shammy's grinder, whether to distract Shammy from the pain or to serve her own selfish purposes, Shammy was not quite sure.

'... *but should Outrages be then further committed by the Natives, on Information being given to the Magistrate of the District, AN INQUIRY WILL BE CONDUCTED TO DISCERN PREVIOUS AGGRESSION ON THE PART OF THE SETTLERS, and should they be found guilty the most active Measures will be taken for the Apprehension and Punishment of the SETTLER AGGRESSORS, in like Manner as under similar Circumstances would take Place whenever British Subjects are concerned ...*'

'That's better,' Maree said.

Shammy sat back up with relief.

'In the last two paragraphs, can you add the word "GRATEFULLY" as many times as you can?'

'I can.'

'*Some few Sacrifices may be required; and it is hoped they will be GRATEFULLY AND chearfully made by the SETTLER, towards the Restoration of Peace; but should the GOVERNOR be disappointed in his ardent Wish for the Re-establishment of good Will be-tween the Settlers and the Natives, minute Enquiries will be made into the Motives and Conduct of*

SETTLER AGGRESSION, and the Aggrieved will receive the fullest Protection, whilst the Fomentors of those Hostilities will meet the most exemplary Punishment. ADDITIONALLY, LAND GRANTS WILL BE WITHDRAWN, ALL APPLICATIONS FOR LAND AND CATTLE AND SERVANTS WILL BE WITHDRAWN, DEPORTATION TO THE HULKS WILL BE COMMENCED AND THE FULL FORCE OF BRITISH LAW WILL BE APPLIED. By Command of His Excellency, The Governor, J. T. CAMPBELL, Secretary.'

'There are no hulks here,' Maree said.

'I know. But the power of the rumour is not to be underestimated.'

As Shammy, free of the piece of duck meat, went back to compositing the changed text, Maree continued to busy herself with the annotated copy of the original Governor's Order at Mister Howe's desk.

'Did you see this?' Maree said. 'Seven idiots thought they could cross the mountains, get to the West Coast, build a vessel and sail to Timor. Needless to say, they got to Emu Ford and then had to turn back, starving, having eaten some of their dogs.'

'I have always maintained, as Emperor Akbar did, that they are "an assemblage of savages". What they did to Tipu

Sultan and his army is only the most widely known of their barbarism.'

Shammy noticed that Maree did not dignify this comment with a response.

When Shammy finished setting the type, she began to print. The thunder of the press as fifty copies came to life woke up Mister Howe's children sleeping upstairs. They were used to these loud detonations as ideas exploded onto paper. They came running downstairs anyway.

'Nothing to see here, children. Your father will be back soon.'

When they still didn't return upstairs, Shammy opened the cabinet near the door, pulled out the bottle of undiluted rum and fed a spoonful to each of them. Satisfied at the completion of a ritual, the children went back to bed.

As soon as Shammy had printed the fiftieth copy, something unexpected happened. It was possibly the result of the constellation of Leo lying very close to the Western horizon, or the Omega Centauri burning more brightly than it had ever done before, or perhaps because he couldn't take any more of the 'Recitation of the Odes'. But in the pulsing heart of that night full of potential, much earlier than expected, Mister Howe walked in with his wife, who went upstairs immediately.

'You're early, Mister Howe!'

Mister Howe smiled at Shammy. 'What are you still doing here?'

Shammy could have said anything and got away with it, so complete was Mister Howe's inebriation that night. In fact, he didn't even notice Maree cowering in the corner. Shammy chose to speak a version of the truth.

'You asked me to finish printing, Mister Howe.'

'Ah. And I thank you for it, Shammy, my dear.'

'Always at your service, Mister Howe. I can deliver to the Castlereagh Street subscribers, if you like, on my way home.'

'Thank you my dear. My ears are still ringing with the Odes. I'm going upstairs to bed.'

'You're most welcome, Mister Howe. I am always your humble servant,' Shammy called, as he retreated into the shadows.

That night, Shammy and Maree dropped off the *Sydney Gazette* to all the subscribers on Castlereagh Street, even those who had not yet discharged their subscriptions. Then they walked quickly to the dense waterfront to pick up the precious box full of premium EAC pashmina shawls and monkey caps. Their porter rostered on for the Friday night shift had delivered it as planned and left it in a secure spot that only Maree had knowledge of. This secrecy was essential, she told Shammy, to maintain the integrity of the warehouse arm of the EAC. Frankly, Shammy was in no mood for such thinly disguised attempts at control. But she maintained her composure and her acquiescence. Trust, or at least the pretence of it, was an essential factor in any business relationship.

But then, against all expectations, Maree said, 'Okay, I'll show you. Come with me.'

Shammy was surprised. The wind dropped to a calm caress. The night, the years ahead, lay before the two entrepreneurs like a carpet of bright winter wattle.

Maree and Shammy retrieved the box and dragged it through the darkness, under the aerial roots of the Birra Birra trees close to the shore. They carried the box together to the approved location where Bhavani was waiting for them as planned, ready to take off to Kirribilli in his secret canoe. Shammy and Maree were slightly surprised by the canoe. It belonged to Aunty Karoo. But they didn't engage in any conversation. Not even when it was clear that he wanted their validation.

'Memsahib Shammy, memsahib Maree, shall I tell you how I was so lucky to find—'

Shammy cut him off immediately. 'Thank you, Bhavani, we are most appreciative of your help.'

They were paying him to be loyal, and to make the appropriate transport arrangements, not to encourage any illusions of friendship.

A few weeks later, the initial outrage had abated. The Governor had been convinced that it was in his own interests to let the changing of his Order go unpunished so he could go back home to Mull earlier than expected. Shammy and Maree began to get used to the new power coursing through them. It took time, strategic thinking and a small forfeiture of natural and unnatural relationships. But Shammy and Maree managed to smoothen out their business processes without any loss of life. The Gadigal felt safe enough to resume the old ways. The land exhaled with relief. Then, when the new settlers stopped arriving and the old settlers began to pack up and move on to a different continent, Maree and Shammy had two separate realisations.

One hot evening when visiting her aunty before the corroboree, Maree saw that the Mankurad mango seed she had stomped on with the force of a betrayed daughter in Parramatta some years ago had grown into a tree by the edge of the river. There were fruits hanging off it. Her aunty told her that the fruits were sweeter than anything she had ever tasted.

'It is as if this tree drinks from the heart of this land.'

That same evening, in Sydney town, Shammy was in Mister Blue's boat. Before she stepped into the boat, she lifted up some of the aerial roots of the Birra Birra trees growing along the water's edge, and carried them with her.

'Let's see if they will reach the other side,' she said to Mister Blue, just for fun.

'Of course they will,' Mister Blue said to her. 'Can't you see how long they are? Aren't you Indians supposed to be good with numbers, with measurement, with profit and loss?'

Shammy laughed, happy in the knowledge that the EAC was thriving. Maybe she could use Mister Blue's contacts in New York to expand the business there.

'The Khasi in Shillong, the Baduy in Java, the people of Sumatra, they have all made living root bridges out of such trees. I have seen them myself. But here, they will put me out of business,' said Mister Blue.

Shammy smiled. A new flame lit up old ideas that had so far remained in the shadows. 'Not here, Mister Blue, but there!'

She pointed further out, to Kirribilli.

Then on New Year's Eve of 1814, Maree met Shammy again, in their usual place under the aerial roots of the Birra Birra trees.

'My father is alive. He will return to me soon. I am sure of it.'

'What makes you so sure, Maree?'

'The mango tree drinks from the heart of this land. Its fruit is sweeter than anything I have ever tasted. It grew from the seed he gave me. What can that be other than a sign that he loves me still? That he will return.'

'I see,' said Shammy, making a note of this explanation to use in next week's Vedic astronomy session planned for her memsahib's friends.

'I want to plant mango trees everywhere.'

'Once we have finished the East Australia Company Bridge connecting Sydney Cove to Kirribilli. It will save us time and money. We will not need to suffer Bhavani. We will need your beautiful Aunty Karoo's canoes to carry the aerial roots from one side to another.'

'On one condition,' Maree said.

'Name your price.'

'We will call the bridge the East Australia Company Mango Bridge.'

It took years from conception to execution, but this is how the East Australia Company Mango Bridge was built. Shammy wanted toll-gates at each end of the bridge. Maree said no. Maree wanted star jasmine growing along the living walls of the bridge. Shammy said no. By the time of the first crossing, Shammy and Maree had children of their own. At the inauguration, the two matriarchs stood on either end of the bridge and performed tree planting ceremonies, using Mankurad grafts brought in all the way from Goa. They walked across the bridge, meeting in the centre, to the sounds of the EAC workers singing the EAC anthem. It was the season for wattles. They showered their blessings upon the

Mankurad saplings preparing to drink from a new continent, yellow blessings sticking in the freshly forking branches. As for the shared oily foreheads of Maree and Shammy, that is a story for another time.

Author note: Thank you to Michael Mohammed Ahmad, Balakrishna Pillai and Elizabeth King for insightful feedback, to Stephanus Peters and Graham Elphick of the Penrith Museum of Printing for detailed information about the printing process, to Jane McCredie for the story of the living bridges, and to Marika Duczynski and Melissa Jackson from the Indigenous Services Unit of the State Library of New South Wales for the story of Cora Gooseberry.

Your Skin is
the Only Cloth
You Cannot Wash

Future D. Fidel

'Your skin is the only cloth you cannot wash,' said the six-and-a-half-foot man seated in the driver's seat of my cab, as he glimpsed his eyes at me. 'Where are you from?' he added.

'I'm Congolese,' I responded, sipping on a can of soda I got from my hotel room.

'I'm Algerian,' he said. 'So, I'm not that different from you; I used to have a friend in my class who ended up becoming a surgeon.' The Algerian man spoke passionately, waving his hands around. 'His name was Mohammed. That man encountered a lot of racism, but on some occasions when the racist was caught, they would get the most vicious beating for their racism. My skin might have been a little bit lighter than Mohammed's, but so what? Maybe he ate a little bit more chocolate than I did; but that doesn't matter, because Mohammed's uncle fought for our country. He saved my people, so, that makes Mohammed my people.'

He went on to talk about the DR Congo and the struggles it had gone through. It was very interesting, to the point where I started questioning my time in high school history classes and the fees I paid to sit in those lectures – whether or not it was a wasted chunk of school fees.

The Algerian man looked over at the Melbourne city-scape which was on our left as he continued telling me stories about his first experiences coming to Australia. 'Another Congolese cabby friend of mine had picked up a few men who wouldn't stop insulting him,' he said, while swerving the car into a faster moving lane. 'Halfway along the trip, my Congolese friend could only hear his passengers in the back saying nigger this, nigger that, so he leaned back to them and asked, "On which one of these poles do you want me to hit this cab?"'

The Algerian man looked over at me and we both cracked out laughing. I could picture myself saying the same thing if it had happened to me, even though I had never thought about it before then. Especially the time I was stopped by the police for working. Oh, yeah. It happened to me.

There I was doing my day job at the time, which was going door to door, trying to convince home owners to put solar on their roofs. Yeah, I don't think there's a job I haven't done. You name any job and chances are, I've done it. I'm pretty sure every high school leaver would also say the same.

Anyways, on one of those days, I ended up on the wrong street at the wrong time. My team leader had just dropped me off in a suburb that I can't name, (Mt Ommaney!) yeah! Fully uniformed with a backpack, an iPad in my hand and my ID badge on a lanyard around my neck.

I knocked on the first door but there was nobody home, so I proceeded to the next house, just as my normal routine. As I headed to the fifth knock, I saw a police car pull over by the roadside. It didn't scare me because I am not one of those people who's afraid of the police. I casually walked to the door but before I could knock, one of the officers asked me to freeze.

I thought to myself, *What an unusual circumstance.* I was there thinking, *They can't possibly be talking to me,* so I continued. Man, did that scene escalate quickly. Before I turned around, there were three other police vehicles on the road. Now I was thinking, *I must be like one of those big criminals to attract this many police cars to my arrest, or maybe the criminal is in the house that I'm standing in front of?* Wrong! I was the criminal.

'Put the bag down,' one of the officers demanded. There was only my lunch in the bag and a bottle of water that I wasn't ready to share. I mean, it was only 11am and when hunger starts knocking, you'll wish you had packed the last loaf of bread you ignored.

'What do you have in the bag?' the officer asked.

'Nothing,' I said. That seemed like a valid response. After all, I had watched a lot of cop shows and I wasn't about to say, 'I have four pieces of bread with peanut butter, a Mars Bar and a one-litre bottle of water.' That would've just sounded weird.

After I had followed their instructions, another police officer came to me and held my hand and tried to put me in the back of their car. I refused to enter until I was told what I had done wrong. I demanded the reason to why I was being arrested. Not only by one police officer, but by the whole Mt Ommaney police department.

'We got reports of burglary,' the officer said. Now I was keen to find out who snitched on the fact that I broke into someone's house and came out with a 55 inch TV. Yeah. They actually told the police that I broke into someone's house and walked out with a 55 inch TV. I was impressed by their descriptive precision, and their incredible vision to know the size of the TV from across the road.

But the officers didn't see a TV on me, did they?

'I shrank it down so it could fit in my backpack,' I said to them. Well, I didn't say that out loud but thinking about it now, maybe I should have.

For the next five hours, I was stuck in a small, cold room at the police station and when the officers came in, they asked if I wanted to have a lawyer present before I confessed my sins. I just smiled and insisted they tell me who was the person that saw me breaking into a house. Yeah, it's always an old white lady who lives alone with her cats. Well, I am not sure if she had cats but I would pretty much assume she did. If not, then she must have had one of those tiny European dogs called 'Tiny'. And of course, even you can assume she lived alone, because I can't imagine two grown people standing by their window guarding their street with binoculars and the husband shouting, 'Look at the size of the telly he just robbed.' The old white lady must not have had anyone asking her to make a cuppa to have all that spare time to herself.

'We're going to tape the interview for our records,' one lady officer said, plugging things into a machine that looked a hundred years old.

'I don't mind, you can record whatever you want,' I responded with a smug face.

'You're a very happy individual, uh?' she said. I think she meant to say, 'You're a very happy criminal, uh?' I just smiled again before she turned around to start asking me all twenty-one questions:

'What were you doing on the street?'

'Can you explain why you broke into the house?'

'This is the second time you've broken into a house on that street, isn't it?'

Second time? Even I was shocked that I'd been there twice. Apparently, all black people look the same. It's definitely something I never knew. How about that old saying, *You learn new things every day?*

I was wearing my smile throughout the interview simply because I was missing work. I mean, I didn't mind the job on the payday, but spending a whole day working regardless of the weather condition just to make it to that payday can be traumatising sometimes. For the first time, I was enjoying my arrest because I could sit under the AC. You wouldn't mind getting arrested either if you were working under a 40-degree heat. That AC would feel like heaven. Although the officer's questions were starting to irritate me. If I wanted to be nasty to that officer and the African in me kicked in, the interview would have gone something like this:

Officer: What were you doing on the street?

Me: Wasn't the street designed for people to walk on?

Officer: Can you explain why you broke into the house?

Me: I thought it was my house. The keys didn't work so how else was I supposed to get inside? Through walls?

Despite the fact that I was trying my best to be nice to the officer every time she asked me a question, my mind always came back to the same response, *Who told you?* I never said it out loud, but I was thinking about it because I was getting angry. *I eat people when I'm angry.* If only I had said that when she kept asking questions.

After hours of pointless questions in that air-conditioned small room, the officers in charge, a man and a woman, voluntarily dropped me home. Now I was sitting in the back of their car getting a thousand apologies. I wasn't offended so we cracked jokes till I got home.

'Hey, how come cops love donuts?' I said.

'Are you kidding me, donuts is life!' the male officer on the wheel responded. Both officers started cracking out, so I cracked out too. 'We use the hole as a shooting target. That's why we don't miss,' the male officer said as he continued laughing.

To be honest, I believed him, till the lady officer leaned back and said, 'We sometimes work long hours, so we have to always be ready for anything. A cup of coffee keeps you awake, so you take a donut along with it.'

All of a sudden, the officers seemed much friendlier than the first time we met, and I was thinking, *Where did you two come from?* I thought to myself, *How about that?* I learnt two things in one day. It all reflected back to the Algerian man's statement, 'Your skin is the only cloth you cannot wash.'

'Next time, they'll respect you,' the Algerian man said, looking down at the red-and-black scarf I had hanging down my neck.

'Do you know what that means?' he asked, pointing at the scarf. I didn't want to tell him I was wearing it because of the cold weather in Melbourne – I was intrigued to hear what he had to say about it so I just kept quiet.

'It means you're welcomed there. Every time you go back to that school, you'll feel welcomed because you have been there before as a guest.'

Of course, he was referring to Scotch College, where I had just finished giving a short presentation about my journey from a small village in Eastern Congo to the big city of Brisbane. I didn't want to tell him that I bought the scarf myself. I knew he had more to say, and I was ready to listen.

'That's the most prestigious school in Australia,' he said, 'and behind it is the famous Kooyong Stadium, the first stadium built in Melbourne for the Australian Open.'

My forty-minute conversation in the cab made me think about whether we'll always have to verify every shade of a person's skin before we can approve of their Australianness, or will we say, 'Australia is like a packet of M&M's – they come in different colours but they all belong to the same packet.'

Message
from the
Ngurra Palya

Ambelin Kwaymullina

To: Australia, 2020*

From: Australia, 2050*

* dates are based on the failed construct of linear time which forms
a dominant point of reference for the iteration of reality to which
this message is addressed

Greetings from the crew of the *Ngurra Palya*
a ship that traverses all of spacetime
The first of many ships
designed by Indigenous scientific literacies
and built with Western technologies

Our crew
is mainly Indigenous
because Indigenous minds
are the most adept
at understanding how to move gently
through relationships
Without such knowledge
it is not possible
to travel spacetime
because spacetime *is* relationships

It is millions of beings
all alive
all conscious
all constantly interacting
A sea of connections
shifting in multiple directions
across multiple dimensions

We sail this sea
led not by a captain
but by an Elder
an Aunty
She guides us
in this work we are doing
to heal the fabric
of our world
of all worlds

There was much discussion
amongst our crew
about whether to send this message
Many yarning circles
over many cups of tea
This message
is not a part

of the work the *Ngurra Palya* was built for
or the work our crew trained for
We are tasked
with the winding and unwinding
of all that was/is/will be
To heal
To balance relationships
It is complex
difficult
our actions radiate out
affecting all that is
We must be wary
of unintended consequences
We do nothing
without process
without yarning
and cups of tea
Aunty likes hers strong
with a lot of sweetness

Some of us were worried
that sending a message
to the world before the change
could skew possibilities
derailing our reality

But we have consulted
with the Council of Holistic Science
They say the change in the world
that led to us
to the *Ngurra Palya*
and to all the other ships
being built in the shipyards
that led
to the on-Country learning places
where Elders and other critical thinkers
teach people how to transform patterns of thought
so they can live in ways
that sustain all life
is coming and cannot be stopped
It is a knot in spacetime
that no one can undo

Those of our crew
born before the change
said we had to reach out
even in a small way
even just through a message
They said, you don't know
what it was like before
The hate

was everywhere

spewed by trolls

in online spaces

The same hate

in newspapers

on television screens

in parliaments

Sometimes disguised

in softer words

longer words

coded

for use in polite company

Sometimes denied

by the very people espousing it

Gaslighting abounded

The hate was always there

daily sapping the energy

hope

spirit

of so many

So we say to you:

this hate

these voices that glory

in privilege
in exclusion
in meanness of spirit
this is not the future
What you are hearing
are the last gasps
of a dying empire

When the change comes
it will have many beginnings
It will not be one big thing
but a lot of little things
Drops of water falling gently
and running together
into a trickle
then a stream
then an ocean
that roars

We will tell you
about one of the beginnings
just a small thing
A question and answer
at a forum
a panel

on Aboriginal policy
Like every other forum
in the world before
Aboriginal people were talking
about the keys to opening up a better future:
land justice
strengths-based
Aboriginal owned and led
trauma-informed
evidence-based
And the government
wasn't listening

A woman in the audience
white
earnest
asks one of the panellists
what she can do
to support Aboriginal people
The panellist who answered
was my grandmother
She told the woman
Stop asking WHAT
Start asking HOW

My grandma said
that over the years
she'd given that answer
about as many times
as she'd been asked that question
which was a lot
But this time
her answer trended
became a hashtag
was listened to
Not by government
who would be the last to shift their position
but by people
at least some
Grandma called them
'good-hearted people'
the ones who came from a place
of respect
humility
genuineness

Stop asking WHAT start asking HOW
made good-hearted people focus
on all the processes
large and small

individual and collective
by which they could embody respect
for Indigenous peoples
including by yielding space
instead of occupying it

In those spaces
out of those processes
came conversations
Different peoples
coming together
sharing knowledge
sharing aspirations
a thousand small beginnings
towards dismantling
settler-colonialism
the context of violence
the originating hate
within which all other hate exists
on stolen land

The distance between
what is
and what will be
is less than you think

It is no distance at all
There is no linear past present and future
Only the now
with all possibilities
enfolded by
and unfolding from
what is
A just world
is not unreachable
It is what's next
You can breathe it
in your next breath
Feel it
in your next heartbeat
Think it
in your next thought

We know
the struggle is hard
the journey is long
but there are so many who feel
exactly as you do
You are all looking up at the same sky
as the world turns through day and night

And hope

like the stars

is there even when you can't see it

Black Thoughts

Pemulwuy

Hannah Donnelly

I had never before considered whether an Aboriginal person could be an Anglophile. Then I came across one, a full-on black Anglophile. I thought being an Anglophile was a kind of paedophile to be honest, which would be an awkward thing to publicly admit so I looked it up later when they left in a cloud of earl grey and spotted dick: it means a person who greatly admires or favours England and all things English. I mean, sure I went through a phase of watching period dramas about rich British ladies yearning for the D, which was a bit of a sadistic habit, but this was a whole other level.

It had me thinking about why more Aussies aren't Anglophilic, blue-blood cockies on their drought-stricken farms love to pretend they didn't come from the UK, even though the Queen's head is all over their money. Australians think more like Americans, only they never had a war for independence, they had wars to entrench the colonial frontier. The Australian Government doesn't know how to talk treaty: Aboriginal sovereignty meets the sovereignty of the British Crown. That is where all non-Indigenous peoples got the apparent right to be here. That is where law comes from. The monarchy. The head that wears the crown. People forget that but I never have. Maybe it's because I don't hang out with many 'Aussies' and maybe it's because Australian identity forgets its place as a territory of the Commonwealth realm.

In another life, it must have been that, I was working as a Research Officer at the Australian Human Rights Commission when I started following the Royal Family on social media and obsessing over their highly edited public appearances for signs of their true alien nature. There have been over fifty visits to Australia from members of the Royal Family since 1867. I don't remember their faces or names, I've got Angloamnesia, but I used to fantasise that one day the Governor-General would be ordered by the Queen to force the Prime Minister to deliver a treaty. Or that a representative would take any of the existing multiple propositions of treaty, like the Barunga Statement, a painted declaration of ownership and self-determination, directly to the reigning sovereign of the Commonwealth for some type of proclamation. That bark painting is still hanging in Parliament House, waiting.

I think the Crown sits smugly on the periphery when we talk about reparations, laughing all the way over in Buckingham Palace at the delusional democracies and feral rabbits left to make sense of their new world. Aboriginal people would still get more out of negotiations with the head of the Commonwealth than with a president of a new republic. I'm telling you, the Sovereign Union was really on to something. They were a group of Aboriginal activists, holding discussions and events about a dusty piece of legislation called the *Pacific Islanders Protection Act 1872*. This was back when constitutional recognition for Aboriginal people was being pushed hard for the first time. My job, aside from looking for evidence of the Royal Family's eyestalks on Instagram, was to go through old legislation and find out if Aboriginal people were legally deemed flora and fauna before the 1967 referendum or if that was simply hyperbolic, a cry to reaffirm the need for Aboriginal people to be counted in the census.

No legislation existed categorising us as animals, but the various state and territory protection acts governing every aspect of Aboriginal lives pretty much amounted to that anyway. From forced removal of children, to where we could live or work as an indentured labour force while wages were withheld, whatever it was, bossman knew best. Get permission to travel in to town, sun-up or sun-down, don't go past the boundary. Yes boss. Every city in Australia has a boundary road left over from an apartheid white people prefer to think of as speculative. It's the only real thing that happened. While I was searching for proof that we aren't plants and combing through old legislation archives, I started to read internal briefs on submissions to the expert panel on constitutional recognition. One of those was the Sovereign Union's submission about the *Pacific Islanders Protection*

Act. This Act legitimised the established practice of slavery in the Australasian colonies known as 'blackbirding'. In a section titled 'Saving of the Rights of the Tribes' there is a glaring recognition of Aboriginal sovereignty:

> *Nothing herein or in any such order in council shall extend or be construed to extend to invest her Majesty, her heirs or successors, with any claim or title whatsoever to dominion or sovereignty over any such islands or places aforementioned, or to derogate from the rights of the tribes or people inhabiting such islands or places, or chiefs or rulers thereof, to such sovereignty of dominion.*

Basically, the Sovereign Union were trying to remind people that the Crown had already acknowledged our sovereignty and ownership of land. I was curious and sent an email to one of the reclusive human rights lawyers on level two, saying, *What implications does this Act have, if any, on questions of sovereignty and native title?* and attached the Act. Before I knew it, the Social Justice team were piled in meeting rooms, pulling all-nighters and writing up proposals for how the Federal Government should disassemble and petition the Queen. The Prime Minister was taking the chopper for clandestine meetings with the Commissioner. Media releases were being drafted and rewritten. Prince William, Duke of

Cambridge, flew in to Canberra to be briefed. He stood side by side with the Governor-General for days of negotiations cutting through the red tape with the Sovereign Union and members of the National Farmers' Federation and Australian Mining Association. Finally, it was agreed regional Aboriginal authorities would receive the licence for all Crown land. The reparations package would cost less that way. A complete national handback was accomplished in a matter of months.

The absolutely putrid smell of my fungus-ridden KeepCup woke me up. I had a new email in my inbox. *RE: Sovereignty vs Pacific Act 1872: Interesting piece of legislation! I haven't seen it before but it predates Federation so it wouldn't stand up in the High Court. Did you find anything on the flora and fauna? Kind regards, Karen.*

Meanwhile, Prince William still can't find Pemulwuy. An Aboriginal hero, a fierce warrior who led resistance battles and raids on the first British settlers. When Pemulwuy was murdered and decapitated, the Governor sent his head to a naturalist Joseph Banks with a note: *Terrible pest to the colony.* Pemulwuy's remains have not been found, apparently his head was sent to the British Natural History Museum in a jar. Ancestral heroes are still waiting to return while the crown sits easy on Her Majesty's head. Our time is a loop. We'll find our way back, before, after.

Afterword

A Timeline
to 2050

Lena Nahlous

Executive Director

Diversity Arts Australia

In her introduction to *Palestine + 100: Stories from a Century After the Nakba*, Basma Ghalayini ponders the genre of science fiction and its relevance to Palestinian writing. She notes: 'The cruel present (and the traumatic past) have too firm a grip on Palestinian writers' imaginations for fanciful ventures into possible futures.'

In situations of oppression, it is often difficult to escape from, or think outside of, the reality of the present day and the burden of the past. But when one is taken outside of the context of the present, the possibilities for change can be immense. In imagining the future, a level of freedom and power is afforded to the imaginer. What seems impossible in the current time and place is made possible. Unlike the present, the future is not necessarily a battleground. Instead, the future is a palimpsest. It is a place where the past and present provide context, but do not dictate the path.

This is the concept of 'prospective futures', which informed the project that led to the creation of this book. As you have seen, the stories in *After Australia* forge a new path, while still bearing visible traces of the world we currently live in, and the world we came from.

Speculative fiction has long been a site of resistance, and the concept for this anthology was influenced by the legacies of writers of colour – Black, Latinx and Cuban feminist speculative fiction, Afrofuturism, and the work of Indigenous and other minority activists and writers – whose radical and intersectional approaches cast light on present-day oppressions and injustices, while writing new narratives of self-determination.

After Australia has its genesis in Arts Front, a project led by Feral Arts, which brought together creatives and thinkers to reimagine and shape Australia's cultural future. In response to that project, Dr Paula Abood and I – as director of Diversity Arts Australia – facilitated two pilot workshops on prospective futures with support from artist and community initiative Frontyard, inviting artists of colour to image alternative futures in a decolonised arts landscape. These workshops informed the larger Stories from the Future project, produced in partnership with the University of Sydney's Dr Remy Low. Over 150 creative practitioners participated in workshops in Canberra, Adelaide, Parramatta, Casula, Footscray and Perth, developing timelines to the year 2050. Many writers whose work is featured in this anthology were participants.

Across all areas of the arts and creative sectors in Australia, at almost every level, Indigenous and culturally and linguistically diverse creatives remain significantly under-represented, despite decades of diversity initiatives. This is a systemic failure, and it restricts growth of the sector, condemning those artists to the margins of cultural life. Recent agitation from creatives, allies, academics and communities – calling out not only exclusionary practices but also cosmetic one-off approaches to diversity – has highlighted the need for substantive change.

Diversity Arts Australia's work is focused on racial equity in the creative sector. Advocacy work in the Australian creative sector is often reactive, addressing deficiencies and gaps such as government funding cuts, imposed priorities, reduced autonomy and voice, and cultural appropriation. It becomes difficult to conceive of social change when justice and progress are often only imagined in relation to state power, and institutional reform acts as a substitute for real change.

Alongside more traditional means of collecting data (our surveys and published reports), Diversity Arts also engages creatives and makers in the research, to strategically imagine an equitable culturally diverse society. We work to transform structures, discourses, practices, audiences and spaces, and to facilitate a critical dialogue via the voices of artists themselves and their art-making practices. In the current sociopolitical climate – with racism and Islamophobia so dominant in Australian politics, the rise of far-right political movements both in this country and abroad, and the phenomenon of racially motivated terrorism – the use of art and cultural expression as means for social change is ever more urgent.

It would be remiss not to speak of the cataclysmic summer of 2019–20, during which Australia saw the devastating effects of climate change: drought, fires, the loss of over one billion animals and entire ecosystems, the deaths of many people and the displacement of thousands more; and the pandemic of COVID-19, which has resulted in racism and discrimination against Chinese- and other Asian-Australians, and others living in Australia who are from Asian backgrounds. Realities like these are reflected in many of the pieces in this anthology, told from the perspectives of writers from First Nations and non-white migrant backgrounds.

To produce this book, Diversity Arts Australia partnered with Sweatshop Literacy Movement, an organisation based in Western Sydney that is devoted to empowering Indigenous people and people of colour through reading, writing and critical thinking. We engaged Sweatshop's founder and director, the author Dr Michael Mohammed Ahmad, as anthology editor, because of his expertise in, and commitment to, supporting culturally diverse and First Nations writers. With the assistance of Sweatshop's general manager, Winnie Dunn, Dr Ahmad curated the anthology and worked extensively with the writers over a period of eighteen months to develop their stories. As the scale, scope and potential of *After Australia* expanded, Diversity Arts Australia and Sweatshop Literacy Movement instigated a formal partnership with the award-winning publisher Affirm Press, who are known for their strong support for, and investment in, new and diverse literature, to deliver the final outcome of this project.

Congratulations and thank you to the writers of *After Australia*, and particularly to Hannah Donnelly for framing this anthology. Thank you to Sweatshop Literacy Movement and specifically to Mohammed and Winnie for your significant work on *After Australia*. Thank you also to the amazing team at Affirm Press, especially Martin Hughes and Ruby Ashby-Orr, for enabling us to give this book the national recognition and readership it deserves. Thank you to our dedicated team at Diversity Arts Australia, particularly Glaiza Perez and Sonia Mehrmand, for your important work on this anthology and the Stories from the Future project, of which this book is a component. Thank you to our Stories from the Future project partners: the University of Sydney, Casula Powerhouse, Community Arts Network, Feral Arts and Arts Front, Nexus Arts, Parramatta Artists' Studios, Peril magazine, Regional Arts WA, Refugee Art Project, The Street and Country Arts SA. And lastly, we would also like to acknowledge the support of our organisational sponsor, Information & Cultural Exchange, who provide a home to Diversity Arts Australia and Sweatshop Literacy Movement.

It takes a village
to write the future....

The team

Original Concept & Executive Producer: Lena Nahlous

Associate Producer: Glaiza Perez

Project Coordinator: Winnie Dunn

Sub Editors: Hannah Donnelly & Stephen Pham

Cover Artist: Josh Durham, Design by Committee

Design and Typesetting: Affirm Press

Publication Publicist: Pitch Projects

Publishing Director, Affirm Press: Martin Hughes

Senior Editor, Affirm Press: Ruby Ashby-Orr

The editor

Michael Mohammed Ahmad is the founding director of Sweatshop Literacy Movement Inc. His debut novel, *The Tribe* (Giramondo, 2014), received the 2015 *Sydney Morning Herald* Best Young Australian Novelist Award. His follow-up novel, *The Lebs* (Hachette, 2018) won the 2019 Multicultural NSW Award at the NSW Premier's Literary Awards and was a finalist for the 2019 Miles Franklin Literary Award. Mohammed received his Doctorate of Creative Arts from Western Sydney University in 2017.

The writers

Claire G. Coleman is a Noongar author whose debut novel, *Terra Nullius* (Hachette, 2017), was shortlisted for the 2018 Stella Prize. Her follow-up novel, *The Old Lie* (Hachette), was published in August 2019.

Hannah Donnelly is a Wiradjuri writer interested in Indigenous futures, speculative fiction and responses to climate trauma. Hannah is currently working at Carriageworks as Curator of Aboriginal Programs. Her recent work has appeared in *Artlink* issue 39:2 (2019) and *Cordite* 89: DOMESTIC (2018).

Future D. Fidel is a Congolese-Australian playwright. Prize Fighter, his debut play, was made in-residence with La Boite Theatre Company and was nominated for a Helpmann Award. Future's first novel, also titled *Prize Fighter*, was published by Hachette in 2018.

Roanna Gonsalves is an Indian Australian, the author of the award-winning book *The Permanent Resident* (UWA Publishing, 2016), published in South Asia as *Sunita De Souza Goes to Sydney (Speaking Tiger Books, 2018)*, and the four-part radio series *On the Tip of a Billion Tongues* (ABC RN).

Ambelin Kwaymullina is an Aboriginal writer, illustrator and law academic who comes from the Palyku people of the Pilbara region of Western Australia. Her work includes multiple picture books and a dystopian series for young adults, *The Tribe* (Walker Books). Her most recent

speculative fiction novel, *Catching Teller Crow* (written with Ezekiel Kwaymullina, Allen & Unwin, 2018), won a Victorian Premier's Literary Award and the Aurealis Award.

Kaya Ortiz is an emerging writer and poet from the southern islands of Mindanao and Tasmania. She is interested in diaspora, histories, heritage and language. Her poetry has appeared in *Scum*, *Peril* and *Verity La*, among others.

Michelle Law is a writer and performer working across print, theatre, and film and television. Her work includes the play *Single Asian Female* and the SBS show *Homecoming Queens*.

Zoya Patel is the author of *No Country Woman*, *a memoir of race, religion and feminism*, published by Hachette Australia in 2018. She founded feminist journal *Feminartsy* in 2014.

Sarah Ross is an Indian-Australian writer, counsellor and law student from Western Australia currently living in the Northern Territory.

Omar Sakr is an award-winning Arab Australian poet. He is the author of *These Wild Houses* (Cordite Books, 2017), and most recently, *The Lost Arabs* (University of Queensland Press, 2019).

Khalid Warsame is a writer who lives in Melbourne. His essays, criticism and fiction have appeared in *Meanjin*, *The Lifted Brow*, *Overland*, *The Big Issue*, *The Saturday Paper*, *Cordite Poetry Review*, and *LitHub*.

Karen Wyld (Martu) lives on the south coast of Adelaide. Recipient of the 2020 Dorothy Hewitt Award for an Unpublished Manuscript, her novel *Where the Fruit Falls* will be released late 2020 by UWA Publishing. Karen has a non-fiction children's book forthcoming in 2021

After Australia is published by Affirm Press in
partnership with Diversity Arts Australia
in association with Sweatshop Literacy Movement

With financial support from Australia Council for
the Arts, City of Parramatta, Liverpool City Council
and Create NSW

With Key Project Support from University of Sydney

Partners and supporters: Casula Powerhouse Arts Centre,
Community Arts Network, Country Arts SA, Regional Arts
WA, Feral Arts and Arts Front, Information & Cultural
Exchange, Nexus Arts, Parramatta Artist Studios, Peril
magazine and The Street.